Graphic Design and Religion

Graphic Design and Religion

A Call for Renewal

Daniel Kantor

GIA Publications, Inc.
Chicago

Graphic Design and Religion: A Call for Renewal
Daniel Kantor
Copyright © 2007 GIA Publications, Inc.

7404 South Mason Ave., Chicago, 60638
www.giamusic.com

Book and Cover Design: Kristy Logan
KantorGroup, Inc., Minneapolis, MN
www.kantorgroup.com

ISBN: 978-1-57999-662-8
G-7098

Contents

Acknowledgments

MANY THANKS TO...

Sara, my love, for your patience and unwavering support. It's what kept me going.

GIA Publications: Alec Harris, publisher, for saying yes to this book and so many other projects. Elizabeth Dallman Bentley, GIA editor, for your finesse.

Kristy Logan, for bringing this book to life through your impeccable design vision, for hanging in there, and for seeing possibilities that only you could see.

St. John's University, Collegeville, Minnesota: the late Frank Kacmarcik, for a lifetime of work that will inpire designers for generations. Mary Shaffer, for opening the door, and for your belief in the project. Wayne Torborg, for such great photography of the Arca Artium works. Brother Alan Reed, OSB, for your steadfast support and responsiveness.

Nicholas Markell, for your amazing editorial insights and challenges. Your life and your commitment to iconic imagery inspire all creatives.

Doug Beasley and Emma Freeman, for getting us through all the photography when it seemed it might never end.

Augsburg Fortress: Linda Parriott, for believing in KantorGroup so many times. We've learned so much from all the projects. Martin Selz, for trusting us with such important work.

Michael Silhavy and Mary Werner, for adding such dimension to the jurying process.

All the clients who support us and give us the latitude to continue growing. You know who you are.

All the designers, agencies, and organizations that responded to our call for entries. The beauty you create feeds so many.

About the Images

WHEN I STARTED WRITING THIS BOOK, I envisioned texts that would be complemented by visual examples from my own firm's portfolio. This seemed reasonable since so many of KantorGroup's designs for its religion clients adhere to the principles discussed here.

As the scope of the book broadened, however, it became clear that the KantorGroup portfolio would be too limited in scope. A more diverse offering of images was required, a collection of works that would better represent a wider range of faith traditions and appeal to a broader audience. We felt it could also encourage interfaith dialogue. Little did I know that this decision would take me on a four-year search for images.

Early on this journey a colleague suggested I feature the designs of Brother Frank Kacmarcik, an acclaimed liturgical designer whose influential works span over six decades. At the time, Brother Frank was in residence at St. John's Abbey at St. John's University, Collegeville, Minnesota. I had the good fortune of meeting with him a few times before his passing in 2004.

The overwhelming support and enthusiasm of Brother Frank are responsible for much of the early momentum needed to see this project through. Upon hearing about my book project, he granted me immediate access to Arca Artium, his personal collection of rare books and prints. The Arca Artium collection is now part of the St. John's University Hill Museum & Manuscript Library and includes a lifetime of Brother Frank's own designs, many of which are featured in this book. I could write volumes about the spare power and timeless beauty of his work, but I'll let his designs do the speaking. Mary Shaffer, the Arca Artium curator at the time, was also a remarkable resource, both in helping me gain access to Brother Frank and in helping me appreciate the depth of the collection and its relevance to my book project.

After two years of research and photography at Arca Artium, the publisher and I felt that featuring works from today's designers and agencies could further deepen the book. But where could one find such works in a reasonable amount of time?

We considered sponsoring a call for entries, but concerns were raised about the costs associated with such an endeavor. Could a book with such a limited audience support such efforts? It was ultimately determined that the only way to offset such expenses would be to sponsor a fee-based call for entries. The entry fees would then be used to offset the event's expenses, which included advertising, database development, cataloging, photography, digital imaging, judging expenses, jury event expenses, and administrative costs.

Ads were placed in *Communication Arts* magazine, and, over a six-month period, submissions were received from all over the U.S., Canada, and even Australia. Every entry was cataloged into a database and prepared for the jury review. The jurying process took place over a two-day period at Hotel Sofitel in Minneapolis. The jurors represented a broad range of disciplines, including graphic design, illustration, photography, sacred art, theology, and liturgy (see the juror info on the following page). Submissions accepted for publication were then catalogued and photographed.

With the jury process complete, we identified any obvious holes in our image mix and made attempts to seek out specific additional works. For example, no submissions were received from the Islamic faith tradition, so, after more research, we acquired designs from as far away as Iran.

Are there still holes in the mix? Certainly. We were hoping to show more worship programs and bulletins. We were also hoping to acquire some Hindu works, but our efforts were unsuccessful. Finally, we would have loved to feature more interfaith works, more presentation graphics, and more environmental signage. But alas, such endeavors could go on forever, and we had promises to keep. I know there are still many great works out there that we were unable to find. Perhaps future calls for entry will be sponsored.

Readers are likely to notice that the Christian tradition is represented through many of the images shown here. This is a reflection of the fact that most of the works submitted through our call for entries came from Christian sources (we openly invited works from all worship traditions). It is also a function of my own worship tradition and client experience.

There is no Christian agenda at work here. However, my own point of view and visual fluency are clearly informed by and grounded in the Christian tradition. It is my hope that readers are able to see this collection as a lens through which they may reinvigorate their own vision for what it means to communicate beautifully.

Daniel Kantor

NOTE: Image credits are used throughout the book. Image titles that end with the symbol "‡" indicate items that were juried. All other images represent works that were acquired through Arca Artium, the KantorGroup portfolio, or through additional research.

Douglas Beasley
Founder of Beasley Photography and VisionQuest Photographic Workshops
As a commercial and fine art photographer, Douglas Beasley's personal vision explores the spiritual aspects of people and place and is concerned with how the sacred is recognized and expressed in everyday life. His works can be found in fine art galleries and personal collections throughout the world. For more information, visit www.douglasbeasley.com and www.vqphoto.com.

Kristy Logan
Senior Designer, KantorGroup
Kristy Logan's award-winning works are known for their strategic clarity and conceptual precision. Her experience includes developing brand identity and design solutions for a broad range of KantorGroup clientele.

Nicholas Markell
Founder and President of Markell Studios
Nicholas Markell has over twenty years of experience in creating ecclesial art. He received an MA in sacred theology and MDiv from the Washington Theological Union in Washington, DC. Nicholas's stained glass windows, iconography, and graphics have received numerous awards and national recognition. For more information, visit www.markellstudios.com

Michael Silhavy
Associate Director of Worship for the Archdiocese of Saint Paul and Minneapolis
Trained in music, theology, and liturgical studies, Michael has worked in parish, university, cathedral, and diocesan settings. His extensive editorial experience includes contributions to music and liturgical art/architecture publications.

Mary Werner
Director of Liturgy and Music, Saint Thomas the Apostle, Minneapolis, Minnesota
As a liturgical artist, Mary has over twenty-five years of consulting experience working with parishes on building and renovation projects and has facilitated seasonal environment workshops locally and nationally.

"To design is much more than simply to assemble, to order, or even to edit; it is to add value and meaning, to illuminate, to simplify, to clarify, to modify, to dignify, to dramatize, to persuade, and perhaps even to amuse. To design is to transform prose into poetry. Design broadens perception, magnifies experience, and enhances vision."

—Paul Rand, *Design Form and Chaos* (New Haven: Yale University Press, 1993), 3.

Origins

BROTHER FRANCIS AWOKE ONE MORNING to the sound of someone knocking at his door. It was the year 1350 and Francis was an artisan in high demand. Known as an *illuminator*, Francis was an artist engaged in the design and production of sacred manuscripts and books. Though he was a monk, many of the illuminators he worked with were lay artisans. The art he practiced, referred to as *illumination*, was not a solitary profession. Rather, it required the efforts of an interdisciplinary team of artisans, scribes, and painters whose talents combined to produce lustrous pages replete with ornate letters, masterful calligraphy, and elaborate illustrations, all of which were lit up through bright colors and burnished gold and silver foils. These weren't just mundane objects Francis created. They were portals to the divine, explorations of holy mysteries that could prepare viewers' minds for the experience of worship.

Francis opened the front door of his studio and was greeted by a patron who was interested in having a new a new book of psalms produced, a manuscript referred to as a *Psalter*. The two sat down for tea, and after a short negotiation a list of fees, barters, and out-of-pocket expenses was outlined. A timeline of two to three years was established, and a few days later a messenger arrived to deliver a down payment.

Francis first set about deciding on a material for the Psalter's pages. Though papyrus was the main writing material of his time, Francis found that his patrons usually requested parchment (prepared animal skin) because it provided the most receptive and stable surface for inks and pigments. In contrast to papyrus, which is usually formatted as a long scroll, parchment books use the codex format, in which separate pages are stacked, bound along one edge, and protected within a sturdy cover. Francis favored the codex format because the proportions of the parchment page often invited comparisons to framed pictures, desirable associations that added even more perceived beauty and proportion to his manuscripts.

Next, Francis made appointments with a host of farmers and trappers. During one meeting, he was escorted to a stable of goats, sheep, and calves whose hides were to be harvested and converted to parchments. The different animal hides provided a range of surface qualities, colors, weights, and sizes. He was even shown some samples of thin, translucent squirrel skins. After deciding upon calfskin parchment, or *vellum*, it was estimated that Francis's order would require the hides of a few dozen calves, and the preparation would take two months.

Francis then set about assembling his team. A typical book project required the efforts of parchment specialists, painters, illustrators, miniaturists, scribes, calligraphers, woodsmiths, metal workers, ink and pigment specialists, toolmakers, leather workers, and bookbinders. Some of his team members had to travel considerable distances at great personal risk and wouldn't arrive for several weeks. Francis was prepared to extend considerable hospitality—a few of the artisans would live with him during the term of the project.

Upon receipt of the harvested vellums, Francis celebrated a serendipitous finding: a few of the sheets had small holes, likely the result of wounds or weakening of the hides from insect bites. Flaws in such expensive material weren't usually welcomed, but, if skillfully accommodated by the scribes and painters, decorated imperfections could add even more depth and mystery to the vellums, a trademark of Francis's work.

While he waited for his team to arrive, Francis began preparation of the vellums. Each sheet had to be scraped, leveled, and polished to maximize its receptivity to inks and pigments. Variables ranging from Francis's own cultural traditions to the inks' gum content were considered when preparing the writing surfaces, and many sheets were sacrificed for testing. Yes, this was painstaking work, but it was worth the effort. The resulting soft, velvety finish of the parchments was the optimum surface for fully connecting quill with vellum, eye with heart, and mind with God.

(*Opposite Page, Left*) Headpiece of blue vine scroll on gold grounds at the beginning of the Gospel of Luke, from **FOUR GOSPELS AND HEBREWS** 12:17-13:25. Eastern Mediterranean, Constantinople, Scribe: Ioasaph of the monastery of the Theotokos ton Hodegon, dated 1366 © British Library Board. All Rights Reserved. Burney 18 f. 101.

(*Opposite Page, Right*) Detail of same book's cover: Gold plaquette on blue velvet over wooden boards depicting Adoration of the Shepherds. Eastern Mediterranean (Constantinople, monastery of the Theotokos ton Hodegon), dated 1366 © British Library Board. All Rights Reserved. Burney 18 upper cover.

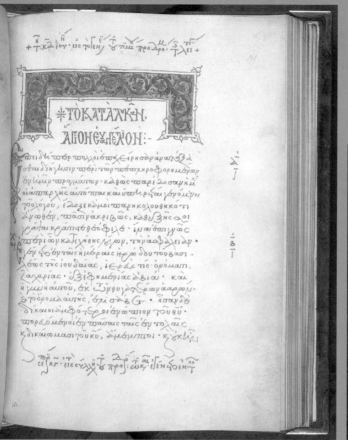

A typical book project required the efforts of parchment specialists, painters, illustrators, miniaturists, scribes, calligraphers, woodsmiths, metal workers, ink and pigment specialists, toolmakers, leather workers, and bookbinders.

Supplies were the next concern: though local resources were used as much as possible, this project required minerals and organics unavailable locally. Many of the supply items came from the four corners of Francis's known world. For pigments and inks he needed lapis lazuli, vermilion, azure, graphite, red sulphite of lead, powdered white lead, and malachite. These materials weren't easy to find and required weeks of investigation, but the luminous qualities they conveyed necessitated their use and justified all the effort. Other tools and supplies included gold and silver leaf, fish glue, pumice, cherry and plum tree gum, gesso, agates, semiprecious stones, hollow reeds, ivory, bone, metal, a variety of animal hair, and quills from turkeys, swans, and geese. Once acquired, the raw materials required further processing and refinement, which took several more weeks.

Perhaps Francis's least favorite part of the job was preparing the fish glue. Used not only as an adhesive, the glue was an effective sizing agent for his vellums. Properly applied, it strengthened the sheets and prevented the inks and pigments from penetrating too deeply. When mixed with ink, the glue also bound the pigment particles together, forming a film over the ink as it dried, an organic barrier that protected the pages from hazardous exposure. Luckily, Francis knew a fisherman who could provide the necessary ingredients: the skin of an eel, the bones of a wolffish, and the air bladder of a sturgeon. All were then simmered with plant gums, and molasses was added as a plasticizer to prevent the glue from becoming too brittle and flaky when it dried.

After months of arduous preparatory efforts, the most rewarding phase of the project finally began: conceiving each page. Francis delighted in the mingling of minds and the synergies of spirit that took place each time his illumination team assembled. A mindful process of prayer and theological reflection was engaged that blurred the lines between prayer and vocation. Indeed, such lines never existed in Francis's world. He couldn't imagine a world apart from the reality of the divine.

The development of each page began with a scribe, who sketched out in hard point (graphite) a framing pattern approximating everything from the initial caps to the flourished penwork and decorative miniatures (small paintings depicting scenes, characters,

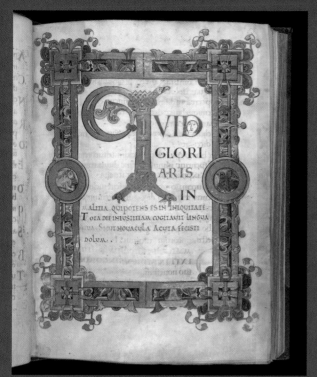

1. When a miniature painting was completed, it was literally cut out from its canvas and pasted onto the final page. Today's *clip art* and *cut-and-paste* techniques are reminiscent of this tradition.

and ceremonial gestures).[1] The page size and grid design used a proportional ratio called the *golden section*, which was said to reflect the divine in all things. Francis and his team were carrying on a tradition that had been virtually unchanged for centuries.

With the sketch work complete, a more permanent inking process followed. To keep the project moving, many of the miniatures were concurrently painted on smaller parchments and then glued into place as each page was completed. With the design finalized in ink, application of the gold leaf began. To help the delicate sheets of priceless metal adhere to the vellum, moist air was applied by gently blowing through a hollow reed. The gold was then burnished to a soft glow using the fanged tooth of a wolf, bear, or boar.

Next came the color washes and calligraphy. Layer upon layer of pigments were built up to reveal a kind of depth that couldn't be conveyed by a single application of color. A delicate choreography between calligrapher and painter began. Image yielded to word and word to image until each page coalesced into a unified whole. It was a communal effort through which the identity of one artist could only be fully known through that of the others. Though Francis encouraged his team to strive for a unified stylistic voice, he understood that each of his artisans was human. After spending so much time with his team he even learned to recognize, through perceptible shifts in their lettering, their changing moods throughout the course of the project. Francis smiled as he gazed at the warm, human quality this contributed to his book.

The individual finished pages were finally ready to be sent to the bookbinder. The stacked pages, once bound, were wrapped with an embossed leather cover that had been studded with brilliant stones and delicate metal work. A few years had passed since work began, and Francis looked forward to presenting the finished Psalter to his patron. He loved his work and didn't take it for granted. While at times stressful and frustrating, illumination was mostly a prayerful, meditative endeavor enhanced by the feel of the vellum, the scratch of the quill, the smell of the ink, and the taste of the hollow reed as it transmitted his breath to the gold leaf.

To Francis, every illumination project was a feast for the senses through which mere mortals could be united with the beauty of the divine, and, indeed, connected with a sense of their own inherent beauty. He felt blessed to participate in this sacred tradition.

(Opposite Page and Following Spread) **KACMARCIK BOOK OF HOURS, CIRCA 1500** Photo © The Hill Museum & Manuscript Library, Arca Artium collection, St. John's University.

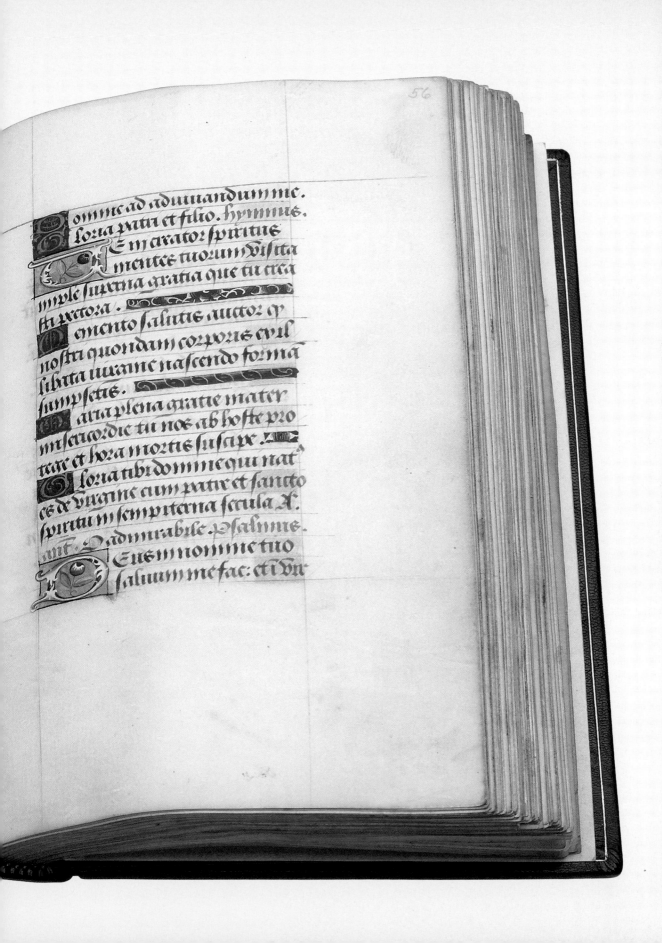

omne ad adiuuandum me.
loria patri et filio. hymnus.
Eni crator: spiritus
mentes tuorum visita
imple superna gratia que tu crea
sti pectora .
emento salutis auctor: q̄
nostri quondam corporis evil
libata virgine nascendo forma
sumpsetis.
aria plena gratie mater
misericordie tu nos ab hoste pro
tege et hora mortis suscipe . X
loria tibi domine qui nat⁹
es de virgine cum patre et sancto
spiritu in sempiterna secula . X .
ant. O admirabile . Psalmus.
Eus in nomine tuo
saluum me fac: et i vir

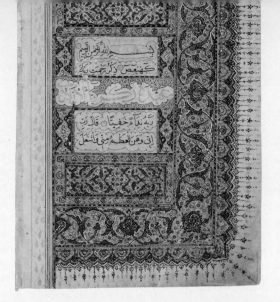

CARPET PAGE Page from a Koran. Courtesy of the Hill Museum & Manuscript Library, Arca Artium Collection, Saint John's University (Collegeville, MN).

THE FOURTEEN AUSPICIOUS DREAMS OF THE JINA'S MOTHER: PAGE FROM A DISPERSED KALPA SUTRA (BOOK OF RITUALS)
ca. 1465, India, Uttar Pradesh, Jaunpur, ink, opaque watercolor, and gold on paper. The Metropolitan Museum of Art, Purchase, Cynthia Hazen Polsky Gift, 1992 (1992.359), Photograph © 1996 The Metropolitan Museum of Art.

ILLUSTRATED MANUSCRIPT OF THE LOTUS SUTRA
Koryŏ dynasty (918–1392), ca. 1340, Unidentified artist (late 14th century), Korea, folding book, gold and silver on indigo-dyed mulberry paper. The Metropolitan Museum of Art, Purchase, Lila Acheson Wallace Gift, 1994 (1994.207), Photograph © 1994 Metropolitan Museum of Art.

HARIVAMSA (THE LEGEND OF HARI [KRISHNA]),
Detached folio from an illustrated manuscript, ca. 1590–95;
Mughal, Attributed to India, Ink and colors on paper. The
Metropolitan Museum of Art, Purchase, Edward C. Moore Jr.
Gift, 1928 (28.63.1) Photograph © 1985 The Metropolitan
Museum of Art.

Religions across the globe and
throughout history have practiced
the art of illumination.

**THE BELLES HEURES OF JEAN OF
FRANCE, DUKE OF BERRY**
1406–8 or 1409 Pol, Jean, and Herman de Limbourg
(Franco-Netherlandish, active in France, by 1399–
1416) French; Made in Paris, ink, tempera, and gold
leaf on vellum. The Metropolitan Museum of Art,
The Cloisters Collection, 1954 (54.1.1) Photograph
1987 © The Metropolitan Museum of Art.

MARY, A MODERN DAY GRAPHIC DESIGNER, just learned that her firm had been chosen to help redesign a denominational book of worship—a hardcover, hymnal-like resource to be distributed worldwide, containing hundreds of pages of ritual texts, images, and service music. The book would one day replace an older version that millions had come to love. Thus the new design needed to honor tradition while still refreshing the content with an eye toward the future. While balancing practical, aesthetic, and theological criteria, her task would be to integrate and unify the efforts of writers, editors, composers, artists, illustrators, type designers, typographers, worship planners, theologians, and clerics into a book that would play a part in building a bridge between human and maker. Since a project of this scope would require the oversight of many committees and consultants and involve considerable logistical and production challenges, Mary was relieved that her client approached her two years prior to the book's scheduled release date.

Mary paused for a moment and reflected upon the immensity of the project in which she was about to be engaged: millions of worshippers would experience the book she designed. It would be in use for decades and contribute to some of the worshippers' most poignant ritual experiences. With a heightened feeling of gratitude and anticipation, Mary sensed that her many years of experience working for a diverse range of secular and religious clients had prepared her for a challenge of this magnitude.

The following week numerous kick-off meetings were held to determine the project's scope. Everything from the book's dimensions to its production materials was discussed. Myriad paper stocks were reviewed, and Mary marveled at the bounty of the earth—the lustrous paper textures and colors available were seemingly endless. Ultimately, the chosen paper stock addressed the need for a smooth, luminous sheet that was also thin enough to keep the book as light and manageable as possible.

It was also determined that the book's hard cover was to be wrapped in a durable leather-like material that would receive both foil-stamped and blind-embossed designs, offering the worshipper a visual and tactile experience. It was thought that a book that was both comfortable to the hand and welcoming to the eye would convey a sense of hospitality to worshippers, who would hopefully turn to the book with increasing familiarity and comfort.

One of the more daunting challenges was the need for visual hospitality. A book comprised of such vast, varied content could overwhelm the worshipper with navigational challenges that could interrupt and impede one's worship experience. The worshippers must, instead, feel welcomed by the design, guided by its clarity and nourished through its generosity.

Mary's team, comprised of fellow designers from her firm, began researching typefaces to aid in these efforts. Her client requested lettering that would be spatially efficient, yet fresh, beautiful, and timeless. The typefaces used in the book must also accommodate multiple languages while offering a range of glyphs for use as navigational and rubric aids.

After a few weeks of research, one of Mary's colleagues discovered an Eastern European type foundry offering a collection of recently designed typefaces that were elegant, efficient, and precise, perfect for a book in which ease of navigation and reference was important. Mary smiled when she discovered that the typefaces were originally designed to aid commuters through the maze of a large European metropolitan subway system. After an online purchase, the typefaces were electronically downloaded and, in a matter of minutes, installed on the firm's network for immediate use.

a a a a a a a a a a a a a a

FONT VARIATION
Each letter 'a' in this sampling of serifed typefaces is set at 45 point. They share a base structure, but each letter has distinct proportions and stroke weights.

Attention was then given to the book's cover color; it was the subject of many meetings, for the color would be the means through which the book would be quickly identified. Careful consideration was given to choosing a hue that would set the book apart yet, at the same time, complement the previous edition. Worshippers had grown to love the color of the older book, and changes to such things were not taken lightly.

Also the subject of much deliberation was the book's cover art, which would include a foil-stamped cross emblem and title type. An experienced sacred artist was commissioned to design a cross emblem, a visual mnemonic that would become the primary identifying symbol of the book. The emblem needed to reflect the proud worship tradition that would be embodied through the book's diverse yet unified ritual contents. Its design had to speak to this with dignity and elegance.

Once the emblem's design was complete, Mary began studying ways to balance it with the cover's typography. For a book of this nature, it was essential that word and image work in harmony, each informing and drawing upon the other. The result would become a symbol of a more integrated worship experience. A similar approach was taken with the book's contents; the same artist who designed the cross emblem produced a number of iconic images to be placed throughout the texts. Each image was imbued with subtle typographic qualities to facilitate further mingling between text and image. The typography, then, served not as a counterpart to the images but as an extension, and vice versa. The hope was that worshippers would be inspired to reflect upon and pray through each image while being seamlessly guided to the book's ritual stories, prayers, and songs.

For both budgetary and practical reasons, Mary's client determined that the book's contents would be limited to two colors—black for standard texts and red for rubric and navigational aids. In a book of this complexity, the use of too many colors could create confusion and distract the worshipper from the content's inherent depth. The challenge was to create a two-color solution that didn't have a low-budget look or feel, a design that suggested mystery and openness. Through experience, Mary had long learned that good design could make a one- or two-color work more powerful than a full-color piece. She readily embraced the challenge and began the process of selecting the specific inks that would be used.

WORSHIP HYMNAL Client: GIA Publications **Design:** John Buscemi
The cross symbol is held by one's hands in this simple, yet elegant design.

It was essential that word and image
work in harmony, each informing
and drawing upon the other.

From standard primary colors to pastels, earth tones, and metallics, the countless ink colors available were a designer's dream. Did the book need a bright red or a subdued dark red? Should the black be warm or cool? Which would be most effective for the worshipper? How would the ink look on the chosen paper stocks? After many meetings, the final black and red inks were chosen. Due to the standardization of printing inks, virtually any printer in the world would be able to mix the inks to the exact shade every time. Mary pondered for a moment how long it would have taken the illuminators to acquire these exact colors, of if they would have even been able to find them.

As the project progressed, Mary began to receive text and image prototypes from contributors across the country. This grouping of talent would never be in the same room at the same time yet would remain connected through the virtues of telephone, e-mail, PDF files, Web sites, faxes, FTP sites, and CDs. Such connectivity, a marvel of the modern world, presented opportunities for bringing together ever-larger circles of diverse peoples.

Once she had collected enough preliminary content to get a feel for the book's vast hierarchy of texts, images, and symbols, Mary began sketching out page grid possibilities. She preferred to start with pencil and paper because she learned that designing at the computer limited her potential to generate ideas. With pencil and paper, she found her imagination was freed. She also learned that this step was essential if the end result was to convey a sense of humanity and enlivened imagination.

As Mary sketched, she strove for grid designs that incorporated intuitive, pleasing proportions, but she remained aware of the need to accommodate both stasis and movement—the end result needed to facilitate the worshippers' prayerful reflections while balancing their need to navigate to interrelated sections of the book. To this end, Mary studied some of the grid designs and navigational techniques employed by masters from the Middle Ages as well as those of many contemporary book designers.

Mary looked forward to finalizing the book's many page designs. This was perhaps her favorite part of the job because her mastery of the technological tools allowed her to harness them in service of her vision. This is where it all came together. Like a musician who is all but unaware of the instrument while making music, Mary's technical skills had been honed so as to focus her energies solely on the creation of accessible, relevant beauty.

As Mary reviewed some of the illustrative images to be integrated into the design, she was struck by the human qualities they conveyed: evidence of the artist's hand was present in each image, and she made an effort to preserve this quality as each image was converted to the digital realm through scanning and retouching. Continual efforts were also made to complement these qualities through the thousands of other decisions made to integrate the other media, texts, signs, and symbols. Mary's process was very organic because it needed to remain adaptable to ongoing content revisions. As each round of revised texts and images was integrated, she began to sense her page designs coming to life. Through harmonious design, each page took on more of the energy and vision of the team's many writers and artists.

Eventually a set of comprehensive page designs was completed and Mary's firm produced electronic proofs that were instantly distributed around the world for review. Through modern communication technologies, the life experiences, cultural worship traditions, and diverse voices of the team were able to gather, weave, and harmonize into a book of textural unity the likes of which the world had never before seen.

After two years of work, the efforts of dozens of artists, writers, and designers were integrated into hundreds of pages of content. The final design, stored on a computer hard drive the size of a deck of cards, was then electronically uploaded to a printer several hundred miles away. Within days Mary and her client were reviewing proofs created from these files. This was the team's last chance to catch any typographic errors or adjust elements of the files before they were prepared for printing.

Mary boarded a plane a week later, charged with supervising the actual printing of the books. As she entered the pressroom to review the pages as they came off press, she took in the aroma of the inks and solvents. It was never experienced as an unpleasant smell—it conjured memories of all the works she'd produced for her clients over the years.

(*Opposite Page and Following Spread*) **EVANGELICAL LUTHERAN WORSHIP BOOK** **Client:** Augsburg Fortress
Agency: KantorGroup **Art Direction:** Daniel Kantor, Lynn Joyce Hunter **Design:** Kristy Logan **Illustrations:** Nicholas Markell (top and following spread), He Qi (bottom, see also p. 12).

Holy Communion

Setting One

Gathering

The service may begin with confession and forgiveness (p. 97) OR with thanksgiving for baptism (p. 97). Either order may be led at the baptismal font.

Confession and Forgiveness

The assembly stands. All may make the sign of the cross, the sign that is marked at baptism, as the presiding minister begins.

In the name of the Father,
and of the ✝ Son,
and of the Holy Spirit.
Amen.

OR

Blessed

The presiding minister may lead one

God of all mercy and consolation,
come to the help of your people,
turning us from our sin
to live for you alone.
Give us the power of your Holy Sp
that we may confess our sin,
receive your forgiveness,
and grow into the fullness
of Jesus Christ, our Savior and Lor
Amen.

One of the following or another confession
Let us confess our sin in the presenc

The assembly kneels or stands. Silence is ke

Most merciful God,
we confess
that we are captive to sin
and cannot free ourselves.
We have sinned against you
in thought, word, and deed,
by what we have done
and by what we have left undone.
We have not loved you
with our whole heart;
we have not loved
our neighbors as ourselves.
For the sake

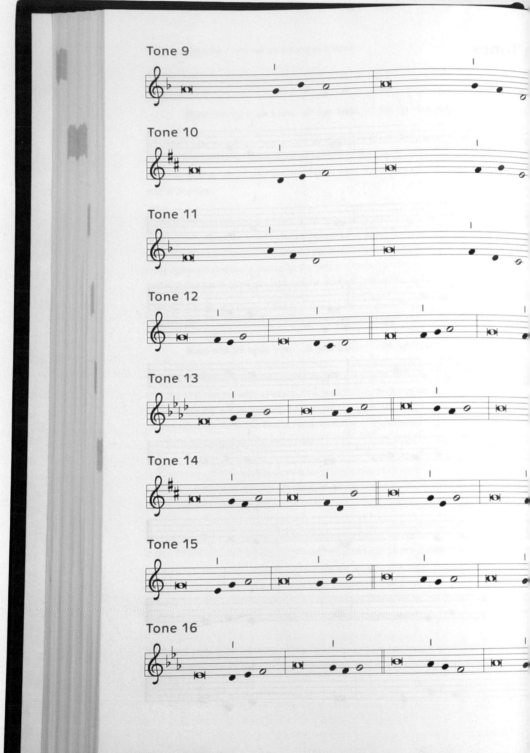

Psalms

re they who have not walked
ounsel ¦ of the wicked,
ingered in the way of sinners,
at in the seats ¦ of the scornful!

light is
w ¦ of the LORD,
hey meditate
od's teaching
and night.

like trees
by streams of water,
fruit in due season,
ves that ¦ do not wither;
thing they ¦ do shall prosper.

so ¦ with the wicked;
are like chaff
h the wind ¦ blows away.

[5] Therefore the wicked shall not stand
   upright when ¦ judgment comes,
      nor the sinner
      in the council ¦ of the righteous.

[6] For the LORD knows
   the way ¦ of the righteous,
      but the way of the wicked
      shall ¦ be destroyed.

2

[1] Why are the nations ¦ in an uproar?
      Why do the peoples
      mutter ¦ empty threats?

[2] Why do the kings of the earth
   rise up in revolt,
   and the princes ¦ plot together,
      against the LORD and
      against the ¦ LORD's anointed?

Despite all her knowledge of the technology, Mary still felt as if something magical happened at print shops, for the presses were able to bring to life and multiply the combined efforts of so many. In a matter of hours, several boxcars of paper were transformed from blank rolls into finished pages that would convey a sense of the beauty and mystery of God. Manufacturing and production equipment from all over the world, technology as sophisticated as any human invention, was put to use in the final production and binding of the book, and Mary remained humbled that her work could be made manifest through such gifts of human ingenuity.

Within weeks Mary received a copy of the finished book. With gratitude, she observed that the end result had taken on a form no one could have envisioned, the beautiful fusion of so many inspired contributors. The book was now ready to take on a life of its own. Through this gift of human and divine creation children would learn to sing, gatherings would be celebrated, wisdom would be shared, tears would be shed, and unions would be blessed. Mary felt humbled to have been part of such a sacred endeavor.

EVANGELICAL LUTHERAN WORSHIP BOOK *See also pp. 19–21.* **Emblem on cover and illustration on spread:** Nicholas Markell

2

Graphic Designers
Inheritors of a Tradition

WHY BEGIN A BOOK on the subject of graphic design with a story about a medieval art form? At a glance, one may be tempted to conclude that the graphic designers who serve religion today have little in common with the illuminators of the Middle Ages. Yet, as the stories in the first chapter reveal, there are significant strategic similarities between the two. A fuller appreciation of this connection can be gained by taking a closer look at both illuminated texts in context and the way in which they were originally meant to be experienced.

PARTICIPANTS OF A COSMIC ORDER

The illuminated text traditions flourished during a time when God or Allah was the focal point of the civilized mind. In medieval times, one's church, mosque, or temple was likely the only place to encounter art of any kind. It is through this exclusivity that aesthetic objects found their potency. During an age when much of the population was illiterate, the power of splendor and beauty to go directly to one's emotions was well understood. The illuminators had a keen and refined sense of the role art played in worship. Sacred images and objects, which today may be taken for granted, had the power to move the medieval worshipper to the "psychic place in which worship occurs." Illuminations were seen as tools that could "focus the senses and the mind and offer a mnemonic aid that gathers the worshipper's strongest and most fundamental ideas, emotions, and memories in an enriched present."[2]

2. Margaret Miles, *Image as Insight* (Boston: Beacon Press, 1985), 9.

3. Miles, 8

The creators of the illuminated texts didn't see their works as ends in themselves but as objects subordinated to a divine framework in which a host of otherwise unrelated objects became "part of the architectural and liturgical presentation of an ordered cosmos of being, reality, and value."[3] Environment, vestments, lectionary, candles, furniture, incense, music, sculpture, stained glass: all were elevated through sacramental unity in which gesture, word, and object came together to serve a single purpose. All these items were unified through a single lens that pointed to a transcendent beyond. To compromise the inherent sanctity of any of the corporeal articles of faith, large or small, would have been unthinkable.

The capacity illuminated texts had to enlighten both literate and illiterate worshippers was well understood by the illuminators. These documents represent a time when communicating through image, symbol, and word was practiced at the highest levels of proficiency and was held to rigorous standards. Illuminated works remind us that worship may be heightened by the mediating qualities of form forged through human hand and prayer. They are exemplars of an age when even the simplest expressions of one's faith were instilled with a sense of sacred mystery and beauty. After hundreds of years, surviving examples of illuminated documents can still inspire us.

Illumination was seen as an act of prayer and meditation through which the divine was made immanent. This reverent union of mind and act yielded documents resonant with human presence and the bounty of God's creation. Through these texts the worshipper could feel the animal hide, take in the aromas of exotic minerals and organics, and encounter the labors of scribes, calligraphers, and painters. The tangible signs of human hand and craft became living symbols of the mortal pursuit for a relationship with God.

The power of strategically unifying an organization's image and the experience this creates for an audience has not been overlooked by today's commercial world. It is called *branding*.

PRESBYTERIAN CHURCH (USA) VISUAL IDENTITY[‡] **Client:** Presbyterian Church (USA) **Agency:** Malcolm Grear Designers

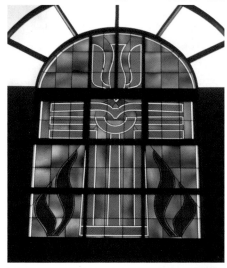

The Cross

The Pulpit

The Dove

The Cup

The Fish

The Fire

The Book

The Triangle

Of course, it would not be practical to expect the ancient methods of the Middle Ages to fully serve the vast communication demands of today's religions. The visual media requirements of modern religious organizations are nothing like they were hundreds of years ago. Graphic design has assumed much of the responsibility for the world's religious visual communications.

When viewed in proper historic context, the illuminators were at the leading edge of the communication technologies of their time. Similar to those working in the graphic design profession today, the illuminators drove the demand for printing supplies; they used the finest tools available; they inspired innovations in printing materials, lettering (type) design, page layout, compositional proportions and ratios, production methods, and even conceptual aesthetic thinking.

Even though the form and output of religious communications have dramatically evolved over the centuries, the purpose and intent of contemporary religious graphic design still share much with the illuminated tradition: both illumination and graphic design demonstrate the skillful fusing of content that balances the seemingly conflicting demands of spiritual, utilitarian, and aesthetic concerns; both convey through tangible media the essential truths and messages of faith; and both represent to their respective eras the use and innovation of highly technical, contemporary communications tools and materials. Just as graphic design is today's predominant printed communication medium, illumination was the principal means of communication for religious manuscripts.

Good graphic design, as all art, is concerned with negotiating the tension between "form and purpose, form and meaning, form and expression, form and content, form and skill. It is the merging of these conflicts that determines the aesthetic quality of a painting, a building, a sculpture, or a printed piece."[4] There is no better place to see examples of this than in illuminated texts. The illuminators conveyed information vividly and efficiently while preparing the mind, through form, to receive it.

Though the term *graphic design* is a contemporary one, its formative principles were hard at work hundreds of years ago in the works of the illuminators. In the hands of skillful artisans, word and image were plied and blended to transmit the wisdom of the world's faith traditions through color, line, texture, and form. A diverse range of styles, points of view, and personalities were conveyed through these documents. The illuminators were just as concerned with opening up the meaning and purpose of the content as today's graphic designers are.

4. Paul Rand, *From Lascaux to Brooklyn* (New Haven: Yale University Press, 1996), 31.

(Opposite Page) **BOOK OF HOURS, CIRCA 1524** **Image Source:** The Library of Congress, Digital Collections

ILLUMINATED MANUSCRIPTS CONVEY TO US TIMELESS VALUES AND IDEALS FROM WHICH TODAY'S GRAPHIC DESIGNERS CAN STILL FIND MEANING AND RELEVANCE. THE ILLUMINATORS...

...saw their work as a ministry worthy of their best efforts.

...believed that God and all appeals to godliness were beautiful.

...believed that to create was an act of co-creation with God by means of the created world.

...understood that prayer could be made more meaningful through deliberate engagements of the senses.

...employed the finest artisans and professionals.

...believed text could be as beautiful as image.

...trained for years and remained lifelong students of their craft.

...unified diverse media from multiple disciplines, people, and sources.

...eschewed shortcuts that compromised aesthetic integrity.

...sought out the finest tools and materials.

...respected the needs of the ultimate viewer.

...created works that engaged both the imagination and the intellect.

...understood and respected the power of symbols.

...came together and worked as teams.

...challenged the viewer to become more visually literate.

...considered their works to be acts of prayer and vocation.

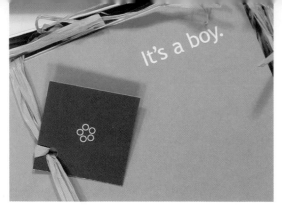

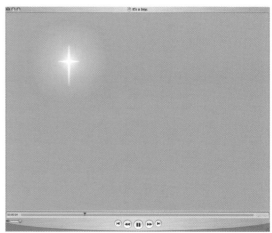

(*Above*) **HOLIDAY CARDS** ‡
Client/Agency: Jager Group   **Art Direction:** Rob Jackson
Copy: Joy Sarnacke

(*Right*) **IT'S A BOY VIRAL VIDEO** ‡
Client/Agency: Jager Group   **Art Direction:** Rob Jackson
Design/Programing: Cliff Wegner

CHRIST BE OUR LIGHT MOSAIC ‡ **Client:** Immaculate Heart of Mary School, Cincinnati, OH **Art Direction/Design/Photography:** Julie Stinchcomb
Illustration: Sarah Wilkinson, Meghan Lemberg, Kelly Wright, Ryan Wampler, Sammy Tucci, Molly Hiltz, Spencer West, Rosie Daly, Brad Kleier, Justin Hebeler, Francine Wright, Hannah Gonce, Rebecca Feldkamp, Abbey Taylor, Christine Mideli, Travis Bromen, Josh Jubak

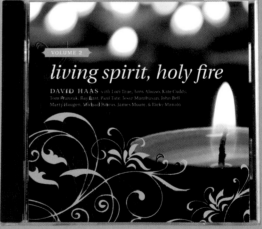

THE FRONTLINE BAND "STILL" CD PACKAGE [†] **Client:** Frontline Ministries **Art Direction/Design/Photography:** David Kasparek

LIVING SPIRIT, HOLY FIRE CD SET **Client:** GIA Publications **Agency:** KantorGroup **Art Direction:** Daniel Kantor **Design:** Kristy Logan

INFANT HOLY **Client:** GIA Publications **Agency:** KantorGroup **Art Direction/Design:** Daniel Kantor

WE COME DANCING **Client:** GIA Publications **Agency:** KantorGroup **Art Direction:** Daniel Kantor **Design:** Jennifer Spong **Photography:** Mike Woodside

SOLI DEO GLORIA CD SERIES **Client:** GIA Publications **Agency:** KantorGroup **Art Direction:** Daniel Kantor **Design:** Jennifer Spong

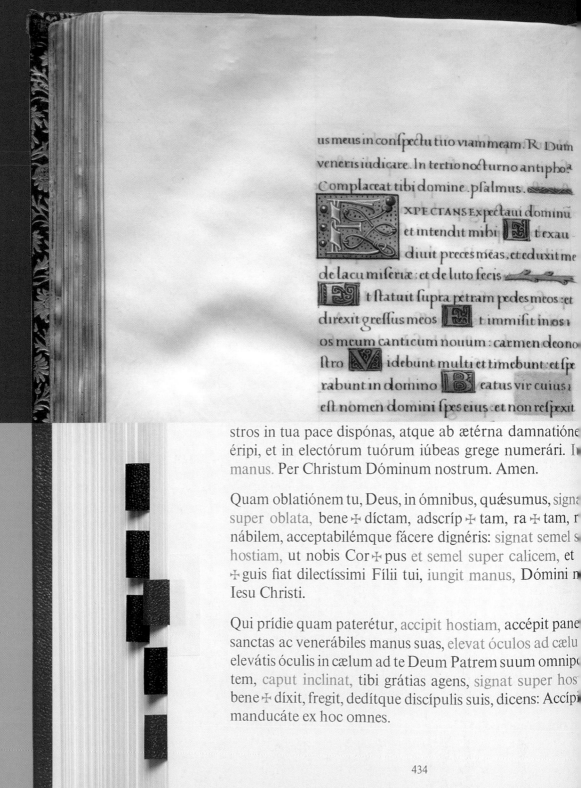

us meus in conspectu tuo viam meam. R̃ Dum veneris iudicare. In tertio nocturno antiphoᵃ Complaceat tibi domine. psalmus. XPECTANS Expectaui dominũ et intendit mihi Et exaudiuit preces meas. et eduxit me de lacu miseriæ: et de luto fecis Et statuit supra petram pedes meos: et direxit gressus meos Et immisit in os os meum canticum nouum: carmen deo nostro Videbunt multi et timebunt: et sperabunt in domino Beatus vir cuius est nomen domini spes eius: et non respexit

stros in tua pace dispónas, atque ab ætérna damnatióne éripi, et in electórum tuórum iúbeas grege numerári. I manus. Per Christum Dóminum nostrum. Amen.

Quam oblatiónem tu, Deus, in ómnibus, quǽsumus, signa super oblata, bene ✠ díctam, adscríp ✠ tam, ra ✠ tam, r nábilem, acceptabilémque fácere dignéris: signat semel s hostiam, ut nobis Cor ✠ pus et semel super calicem, et ✠ guis fiat dilectíssimi Fílii tui, iungit manus, Dómini n Iesu Christi.

Qui prídie quam paterétur, accipit hostiam, accépit pane sanctas ac venerábiles manus suas, elevat óculos ad cælu elevátis óculis in cælum ad te Deum Patrem suum omnipo tem, caput inclinat, tibi grátias agens, signat super hos bene ✠ díxit, fregit, dedítque discípulis suis, dicens: Accípi manducáte ex hoc omnes.

434

PRESERVING THE PURPOSE

Today it is difficult to encounter illuminated manuscripts in the same way their makers meant for them to be experienced. It is easy to forget that these rare documents were to be held in one's hands, touched, and engaged because we so often find them under glass. We may neglect to see them as aids to prayer and reflection because we will likely never be alone with them. Viewers may never know why these documents are relevant to contemporary worship or why so much work went into them because the focus is so often placed on the intrigue of the materials, tools, and techniques used.

Mere reproductions of high-profile illuminated texts can generate millions of dollars in revenue. The tensions created by such commercial attention can detract from the humility and generosity bestowed in their making. It is understandable that a handcrafted work made of real parchment foiled with twenty-four-karat gold may captivate a viewer. However, illuminated texts were never meant to be investments, objects of fascination, or exercises in nostalgia. The illuminators did not intend for their works to be gawked at.

One's focus is ill placed when it romanticizes the sobering, labor-intensive methods of the illuminators. There is nothing glamorous about preparing parchments or boiling fish glue. The purpose of producing these beautiful works was not to call attention to their novelty but to serve the needs of the worshipper through a process of prayer made manifest. One chose gold leaf or lapis lazuli because it was the best medium of the time to fully reflect the luminosity and depth of the message. These choices were made in genuine service of God and the worshipper. There would have been no other reason to use such materials and methods.

When we view religious works in isolation from their intended purpose, we run the risk of losing touch with their power to inform and stir us. By viewing illumination today as glamorous or lucrative, we are in danger of distorting its original intent. We may also be suggesting that other media are of lesser value. With respect to present day communicators, if illumination is seen as set apart from the contemporary art form of graphic design, we risk relegating the art of illumination to the status of museum artifact, and graphic design becomes a mere production medium valued only for its convenience or efficiencies. For both art forms to find a meaningful place in worship today, the two must be seen as intimately related.

(*Opposite Page, Top*) **BOOK OF HOURS, CIRCA 1524** **Image Source:** The Library of Congress, Digital Collections

(*Opposite Page, Bottom*) **ROMAN MISSAL, 1964** **Client:** National Catholic Welfare Conference, Inc. **Design:** Frank Kacmarcik

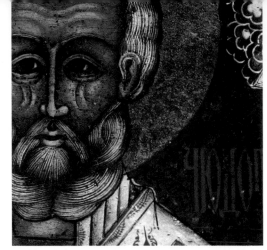

"PSALMS" SERMON SERIES ‡ **Client:** Fellowship Bible Church
Agency: Fellowship Bible Church Media Department
Art Direction/Design: Lynette Behrendt   **Photography:** Mike Bowden
Illustration: Nancy Dunaway (L) and Deborah Allen (R)

HOLY ICONS OF MOTHER RUSSIA ‡ **Client:** Knights of
Columbus Museum, New Haven, CT   **Agency:** Spagnola & Associates
Art Direction: Tony Spagnola   **Design:** Rachel Oliver, Renee Shiller
Photography: David Sundbert, Esto, NY

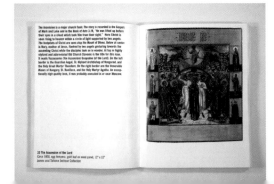

LAUREL/IVY, MANDORLA

CROSS

HOST

SUN, KINGSHIP

ORGAN STENCIL GRAPHIC [‡] **Client:** First Presbyterian Church of
Highlands, NC **Agency:** Huie Design, Inc. **Art Direction:** Sarah Huie Coleman
Design: Michelle Scott **Photography:** Michelle Schwarz

This book is not a call for a return to ancient ways. The complexity and variety of today's religious communications cannot be fully served by quill and ink. It is an appeal, however, to consider the illuminators as the graphic designers of their time. It is a call for a renewal of attitude and spirit, an invitation to revisit the assumptions today's graphic designers make about what it means to communicate with and through faith. If graphic designers fail to see illumination as a living art form that still offers timeless insights, something deep and profound will be lost, for the world craves beauty and meaning more than ever before. Graphic designers in service of religion have much to learn from the illuminators; their wisdom still has relevance.

The popularity of illuminated texts demonstrates that humans still crave what these documents have to offer, but graphic design is rarely seen as a medium that can feed much of this hunger. And no matter how accurate a reproduction of an illuminated text may be, it will always be viewed as inferior to the original. Graphic design, on the other hand, is a medium that reaches its fullest potential not before but after reproduction. It is the medium best equipped and adapted for the high-volume production demands of today. Today's graphic designers need not produce works that look ancient. This is not the point. They are called to explore ways in which their contemporary efforts may be informed by a rich tradition still alive and with us.

Today's religious communicators are encouraged to see graphic design as both a descendant of illumination as well as its present day soulmate. The works of the illuminators can remind graphic designers that through aesthetics the elements of hand, eye, word, symbol, and image become subordinated to a higher order. They teach us that content alone is incomplete without form. They teach us that the communications of one's faith are still worthy of our best efforts and brightest talents. They teach us that the hospitality of visual grace can become prayer for both maker and viewer. Both illumination and graphic design have distinct qualities to offer, and when in dialogue they may result in works that pass on the wisdom of tradition and beauty through a fresh, powerful new voice.

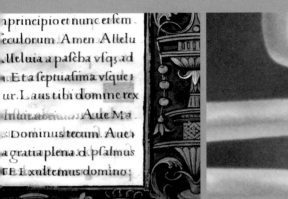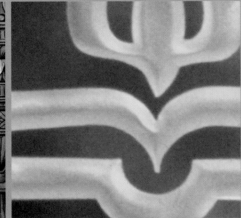

"It is necessary to understand history, and he who understands history knows how to find continuity between that which was, that which is, and that which will be."

— Le Corbusier

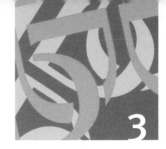

The Need for Renewal

GRAPHIC DESIGN IS A POWERFUL MEDIUM that will have an increasingly important role to play in religion, faith, spirituality, and worship. There is, however, a need for a closer look at this art form that draws upon proud traditions. Religions must begin to see graphic design not as an expensive luxury or an unnecessary frivolity but as a steward of goodwill. Of course, design with no strategic context or no immediate relevance may be experienced as superfluous or meaningless. But when the best plans are laid and the task at hand involves communicating, graphic design is the medium through which the resulting messages will likely take root.

Arguments are sometimes made against the strategic use of design within religion on the premise that religion must not be concerned with the superficial material world. To remain rooted in one's relationship with God, the argument asserts, one must not dwell on how things appear at the surface. Rather, it is the inner depth of one's relationship with the divine that matters. Similar contentions suggest that the excessive sacramentals, ephemera, and illuminated manuscripts of the medieval church constituted an abuse of power and resources that should have been directed in more meaningful ways.

At a glance, the simplicity and elegance of these arguments may appear compelling. But unless argued by an ascetic living the most austere of monastic lifestyles, the above arguments border on hypocrisy. To dismiss the illuminated manuscripts would be an argument against the mosaics of the Orthodox Church, the Byzantine frescoes, French cathedrals, medieval wall paintings, Michelangelo's *Pieta*, the paintings of the Renaissance, the sacred works of Bach, Mozart's Requiem, and Tallis's motets. The culmination of this logic would be the stripping away of the literary beauty of the holy books.

We might ask: *why not just distill holy writings down to the bare facts?* Yet the reason we don't strip these books down to the facts is that we intuitively know we need and deserve more. We are called not just to survive but to grow and thrive. We are called to participate in our own beauty. There is a reason religions celebrate the timeless voice of the Hebrew Scriptures, the poetic grace of the psalms, the deceptive simplicity of the parables, the mystic wisdom of the Koran, and the proportion and shape of the Gospels. Indeed, the Gospel of John is considered by many to be one of the world's greatest works of art. Where would these stories be without the nourishing beauty of their forms? In this light how can any faith-based organization of good conscience embrace music, scripture, or architecture yet fail to care about the visual hospitality of its own messages? How can we not care about how the sublime beauty of a personal relationship with the divine is communicated to the world?

The illuminators set a much-needed precedent for today's designers because contemporary religious organizations often neglect to communicate beautifully. The vast communications media and printed pieces that come out of our churches, synagogues, temples, schools, religious publishers, and faith-based businesses are often mediocre and sometimes profoundly ugly. Modern worshippers and outside observers have almost come to expect the visual communications of today's faith-based organizations to be rife with predictable clichés and abused symbols. The desire for faith-based organizations to communicate to a broad range of sensibilities may even result in the deliberate dumbing down of aesthetics so as not to appear too sophisticated — *we can't look too good or we'll raise eyebrows.* The result? The naive desire for no design inevitably leads to poor design, and the expectations of today's viewers of religious communications have never been lower.

While many other arts flourish within modern religion, the virtues of graphic design are often overlooked. There is a disturbing systemic ignorance of graphic design and its potential to play a key role in elevating the communications of contemporary religion. This failure to recognize graphic design as a true specialty worthy of professional oversight is behind much of the mediocrity in religious communications design.

While people gather to worship in sublime spaces filled with mystery and awe, they are often greeted by trite signage; they are handed poorly designed worship aids; superficial logos and inane symbols are used to represent faith communities that claim rich, authentic traditions; publications such as newsletters, bulletins, and catalogs are known

"Works of art not only satisfy the senses, they bring insight and challenge."

— Richard Harries, Bishop of Oxford, *Art and the Beauty of God* (New York and London: Mowbray, 1993), 23.

(Opposite Page) **ST. MICHAEL CATHOLIC CHURCH, ST. MICHAEL, MN**

From architecture to stained glass, sculpture, textiles
and iconography, many art forms flourish within
modern religion. So, too, must graphic design.

more for their use of kitschy clip art and amateur typography than for the integrity of their content. Such abuses do more than trivialize what is being conveyed. They alienate those who are able to experience a full faith life in which the hospitality of beauty is an essential component.

Faith-based organizations often have conflicting views of graphic design, due in part to the art form's strong ties to pop culture and advertising promotions. It's easy to indict an art form that has strong commercial connotations, one that has seeped into every crevice of our visual experience. As a result, graphic design is an art form that's often devalued or dismissed as nonessential. "*We can't look too slick or corporate*" or "*We're a church, not a business*" are sentiments often expressed by religious organizations as they reflect on image or identity. But faith-based organizations that emphasize their differences from the secular commercial world often neglect to notice and admit to the similarities. The modes of communication used by a business and a church, for example, are virtually identical. The fact that graphic design is so associated with commercialism should not be cause for its dismissal. It is the output, not the art form that must be judged.

There was once a time when worshippers had an uncompromising expectation of beauty in their material expressions of faith. A thousand years ago, it was rare to encounter secular books, art, or architecture that surpassed the beauty found within religion. Yet often just the opposite is true today. The messages and visual communications of the commercial world are doing a much better job of leveraging the strengths of good communications design than are those of religion.

What happened? Are the desires to communicate the truths and ideals of one's faith tradition any less relevant than they were in the Middle Ages? Do we no longer have the will to convey the beauty of our beliefs? Do we no longer desire to share this beauty with others? Does the power of beauty to prepare the human mind and heart for worship no longer exist? Must the mandate for a beautiful outcome be reserved for our highest profile efforts or our most expensive financial outlays?

A meaningful renewal of religious graphic design will require heightened awareness and respect of this art form, but something elemental must happen first: the art form must be *named*. It is easier to dismiss or abuse something when it has not been formally acknowledged.

LOUISVILLE SEMINARY[‡] **Client:** Presbyterian Church (USA) **Agency:** Malcolm Grear Designers

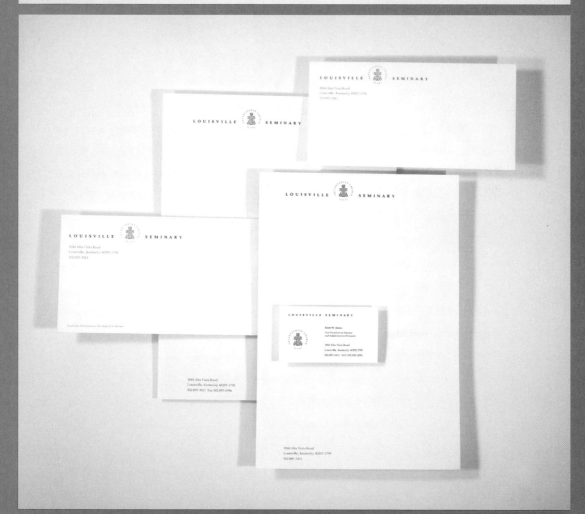

PARK AVENUE UNITED METHODIST CHURCH STATIONERY SYSTEM ‡ **Client:** Mark Horst, Park Ave. United Methodist Church
Agency: Laurie DeMartino Design   **Art Direction:** Laurie DeMartino   **Design:** Laurie DeMartino, Zack Custer

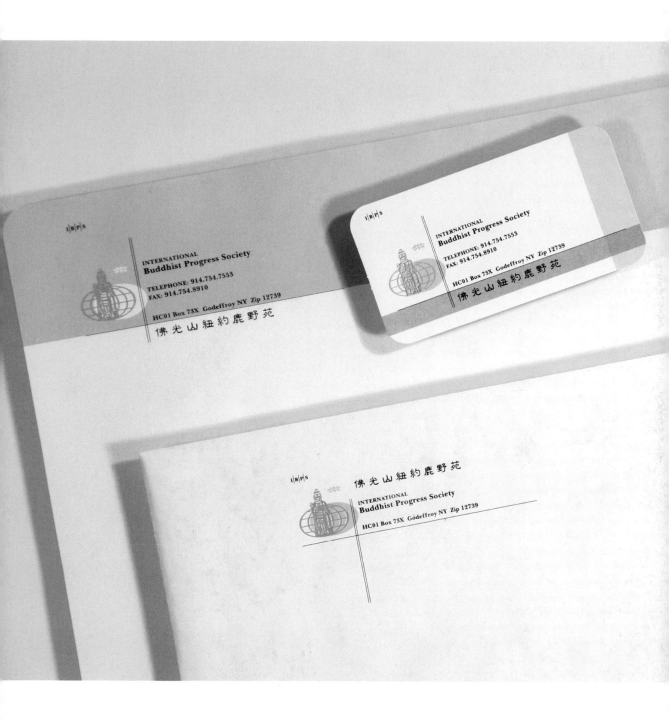

BUDDHIST PROGRESS SOCIETY STATIONERY SYSTEM ‡ **Client:** Buddhist Progress Society
Agency: Laurie DeMartino Design   **Art Direction/Design:** Laurie DeMartino

ST. MARY BayView ACADEMY

SPONSORED BY THE SISTERS OF MERCY

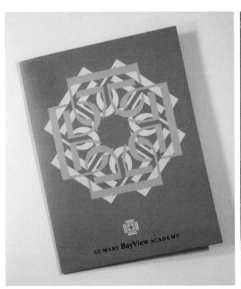

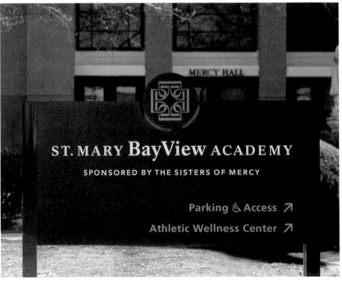

ST. MARY BAYVIEW ACADEMY VISUAL IDENTITY‡ **Client:** St. Mary BayView Academy **Agency:** Malcolm Grear Designers

Catholic News Service

CATHOLIC NEWS SERVICE VISUAL IDENTITY‡ **Client:** Catholic News Service **Agency:** Malcolm Grear Designers

Much has been written on the importance of other art forms in religion and their roles as mediators in the human religious experience. Libraries are filled with books written about sacred music, painting, and architecture. Yet while these art forms thrive within modern worship, the virtues of graphic design remain little celebrated. Rarely, if ever, has graphic design been formally called out as an essential art form of contemporary religious expression. We live in an age when new modes of communication are introduced at an alarming rate, and these media heavily rely on graphic design for their effectiveness. The question is not whether graphic design has a place in religious communications but whether religions, worshippers, and faith-based organizations are aware of graphic design's increasing presence, its strengths, its influences, and its vulnerabilities.

Arguments have been made that spending too much time crafting a faith-based message is one step closer to branding God. Yet such arguments fail to alleviate the vast challenges of today's communications realities or to do away with the responsibilities of elevating contemporary religious messages. Organized religions since the beginning of civilized times have been evangelizing with beautifully prepared messages of reverence, as demonstrated by the illuminators. As long as religion has something to say, it will be doing so in part through creations of the physical world granted to us. Design is the means by which our experience of the physical may be enhanced and the means through which the physical may participate in the metaphysical. Design is a potent delivery vehicle that is able to negotiate the intellect as well as the imagination, both of which are essential to a fulfilling faith life.

"We can no longer accept that the 'appearance' of religion is inconsequential to the 'experience' of religion...it is through the visible world that the invisible world becomes known and felt."

—Colleen McDannell, *Material Christianity* (New Haven: Yale Univ. Press, 1995), 272.

HAND FAN STUDIES Agency: KantorGroup Design: Kristy Logan

"During the Depression, we lived at Morton Chapel Community, and we would walk to Fellowship. If we started a little early, with our Sunday dresses on and shoes and socks in hand, we could make it to the morning service. It was hot weather! When we got in sight of the church, we stopped, wiped most of the dust from our feet, and put on our shoes and socks. There was no air conditioning. All the doors and windows were open. To supplement the cool breeze, hand-held fans were kept busy. Some of the older ladies made fans from palmetto leaves that they had cut and bound. The rest had to use homemade fans. Some of the places of businesses would issue fans with advertising on the back and a pretty picture on the front."

—Mrs. Sammie Elliot, Fellowship Baptist Church congregant, Lamar County, Alabama

Many faith-based organizations are concerned with increasing memberships or raising awareness within their communities. Such outreach initiatives can project a sense of an organization's worship traditions, rich stories, and spiritual relevance. It is dishonest to hide the beauty of these truths. The mindful crafting of any faith-based organization's communications media must include a sense of the sacred, the divine, the holy. To deny this of ourselves is to deny the very qualities that allow us to become more like God. To hide the vivid beauty of one's core beliefs for fear of appearing superficial is to deny the presence of many gifts. It is to deny the recipient of a message that is true and healing. It is to deny the gift of an art form within our midst, ready to assist. It is the failure to come together, to unify around a common voice that is able to say *welcome* with a spirit of grace and dignity. If good design is about communicating effectively through content wrapped in form, churches were doing this long before the commercial world discovered the power and goodwill of design.

Religions are struggling with how to preserve their timeless messages in a self-help, new-age society that has grown to mistrust organized faith. Graphic design must be seen as a catalytic tool for unifying, clarifying, inspiring, and illuminating. Too often graphic design is used not to challenge, educate, and elevate but to perpetuate banal clichés and to mimic commercial shortcuts that have become substitutes for our spiritual sustenance. Until graphic design is named as a critical medium for the health and vibrancy of religion, these abuses will continue, and perceptions will decline. How might this be prevented? How can we see anew the potential before us to view graphic design as a vehicle for the sacred? A first step is to address an age-old distinction: *sacred* versus *secular*. It is here that seeds of lasting renewal can be planted and take root.

"It is the continual interaction with objects and images that makes one religious in a particular manner."

— Colleen McDannell, *Material Christianity*, 2.

YOUNG WOMEN'S RESOURCE ROOM ‡ **Client:** Young Women General Presidency **Agency:** The Church of Jesus Christ of Latter-day Saints **Art Direction:** David Vandivere **Design:** Stephen Tuft

4

The Sacred
and the Secular

IN TODAY'S MULTICULTURAL CONSUMER WORLD, lines are
often blurred between religion, entertainment, and health. Restaurants are built around
Zen Buddhist themes; spas offer meditative healing and spiritual guidance; and many
places of worship now include elaborate musical soundstages, coffee shops, and bookstores.
Even televised worship services are punctuated by commercials. At a glance, one might
conclude that this merging of faith and everyday life is the realization of the Buddhist
ideal in which all things are to be considered sacred.

We also live in a society that is overwhelmed by secular influences and exploitation. It
is a world that encourages consumption, passivity, and self-centeredness, a global economy
obsessed with control and environmental dominance. As attempts are made to sanctify
the secular, powerful forces may instead result in just the opposite: the secularization of
the sacred. Graphic design as it pertains to religion is an art form that is particularly vulnerable to these influences.

There was a time when art was primarily considered a link to a broader ritual life.
"Art had a definite function. And this function rooted it in and orientated it towards a
higher, sublime realm. This spiritual functionalism inspired rather than shackled art,
keeping it timeless, therefore always new."[5] Times have changed, however. Art is now
viewed through a much more materialistic lens. It is seen as something that can entertain

5. Aidan Hart, Iconographer, Assistant Illuminator for the St. John's Bible, "The Icon and Art," (accessed at www.aidanharticons.com). From a talk given at the School of Economic Science, Watterperry, Oxford, March 2000.

us, amuse us, or provide us with an aesthetic experience. Today's secular art is subordinated to the needs and wants of the market, or the customer's taste, or an artist's personal vision. These are healthy tensions for a pluralistic, market-driven economy. We may be losing touch, however, with our capacity to see art as something more, a means to reconnect one's spirituality with the realms of daily functional living. This is the humble, simple power of sacred art.

Graphic designers serving religion today have the responsibility of appreciating what it means to create sacred art. The material efforts of sacred artists remind us that we exist in an incarnate world that is an extension of something beyond us. The tangible, material expressions of sacred artists are means of communion with creation. They show us that through creation we may experience the spiritual and that the spiritual may find and touch us through creation. "The impulse to discover the holy in the corporeal experience of one's physical environment is a universal phenomenon, rooted in the human manner of being-in-world." [6] To suggest that ritual living requires the dismissal of the material realm is to deny the divine purpose of one's own incarnational form. Seen in this light, graphic designers have the same opportunity as other artists to participate in human expressions of love for God, world, self, and others. Graphic design, when practiced within a particular framework, may indeed be considered a sacred art.

6. Belden Lane, *Landscapes of the Sacred* (New York: Paulist Press, 1988), 188.

The word *sacred* is in casual use today. To many, there are no meaningful differences between what may be considered *sacred* or *holy* and what may be considered *special, valuable, important,* or *precious.* Yet when distinctions such as these can no longer be made, something is lost. One's acuity to reflect upon nuances of the truly sacred becomes limited, the ability to create sensate encounters of the divine is stunted, and we lose touch with our need to experience creation in a way set apart from the tensions, stress, and pervasive ugliness of the world.

Artists who create sacred art are called upon to illuminate and amplify the sacred in a world that needs help seeing it. It would be hard to imagine work that is more vital to the future of this planet, for a world that is unable to discern the divine essence of creation is sure to exploit it. Graphic designers who are charged with the mission of conveying religion's messages have the awesome responsibility of opening the eyes of a world that is often blind to beauty and to the divine cosmos.

FAITH AND VISION BOOK[‡] **Client:** Square Halo Books, Inc. **Agency:** World's End Images **Art Direction:** Ned Bustard

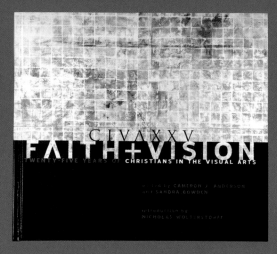

CIVAXXV
FAITH+VISION
TWENTY-FIVE YEARS OF CHRISTIANS IN THE VISUAL ARTS

edited by CAMERON J. ANDERSON
and SANDRA BOWDEN

introduction by
NICHOLAS WOLTERSTORFF

STEPHEN DE STAEBLER *Winged Guardian Victory* 64" × 34" × 24" 1993

WILLIAM CATLING *A Life Span Beyond the Heart Ceremony* covers wood and fabric 62" × 9" × 9" 1995

ERIC DABER *The Temple Curtain, from Veil Top to Bottom* wood 72" × 8" × 8" 1997

JANET McKENZIE *Adam and Eve* oil on canvas, 42" × 54" 2005   HANS DAVID-WEST *African Market* acrylic on canvas, 38" × 48" 1998   JOAN WOLTER *Iris* oil on Masonite 50cm and gilding 40" × 30" 2005   CHRISTOPHER AIKEN *Icon of Isaiah* modified encaustic 30" × 24" (catalog panel) 2002

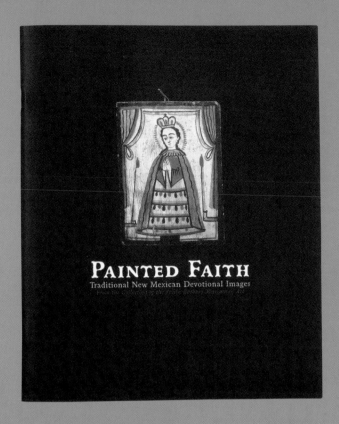

PAINTED FAITH CATALOG[‡] **Client:** Westmont College Reynolds Gallery **Art Direction:** Scott Anderson, Cody Hartley
Design: Scott Anderson **Copy:** Cody Hartley **Photography:** Scott McClaine

EXCAVATING THE IMAGE CATALOG[‡] **Client:** Westmont College Reynolds Gallery **Art Direction:** Scott Anderson, Wayne Forte
Design: Scott Anderson **Copy:** Karen Mulder, Wayne Forte **Illustration:** Wayne Forte

{ EXCAVATING THE IMAGE }

BIBLICAL SUBJECTS BY WAYNE FORTE

BERNARD GALLERY ⁓ WESTMONT COLLEGE
AUGUST 28TH–OCTOBER 18TH, 2003

CRUCIFORM PIETA
1992, ACRYLIC ON PAPER ON BOARD, 96 X 60 INCHES

The idea here was to indulge a very human impulse: to embrace and comfort Christ as He hung on the cross. Artists traditionally used the pieta configuration to portray humanity's grief at Christ's death and I wondered if I could stretch out here the cross. I purposely kept the figures dark so the cross would also read abstractly as a group of modules in cruciform from a distance. My hope was that the viewer would be momentarily disoriented as she approached the piece and was confronted by humanity and divinity embracing on the cross.

CAIN AND ABEL (AFTER RUBENS)
1993, ACRYLIC ON CANVAS, 72 X 48 INCHES

I used Rubens's image of Cain fighting Abel, simplifying it to represent an elemental struggle between good and evil. Pointillistic patter the canvas at regular intervals, making the sacrifice that would one day render this battle.

OBJECTS FROM THE PASSION
1995, ACRYLIC ON CANVAS, 77 X 77 INCHES

This work was inspired by similar texts that I saw in Italy—an array of objects reminding the viewer of the crucifixion of Christ. I simply laid these graphic-like images over a collage of postcards, my childhood drawings, receipts from stores, fingernail sketches and other reminders of my everyday existence, hoping to create a resonance between the two realities.

...AND PETER WEPT
1995, OIL ON CANVAS, 60 X 40 INCHES

The image of a rooster, simply and straight-forwardly rendered, provides the context for the scriptural fragment below it. Setting up a dialogue between the viewer's initial visual perception and the deep emotions elicited by the text when Peter's propensity for jumping headlong into situations before considering the implications.

To experience the sacred is to become aware of a wondrous power breaking through the ordinariness of the world, a presence that has the power to nourish, guide, and heal. But to encounter the sacred requires an imagination capable of affirming the presence of the holy. Unless one's mind is vigilant and open, the sacred can easily be missed. Graphic design, like so many other art forms, can aid worshippers in their awakenings to the sacred. It is a medium through which otherwise plain texts and images may be cleansed and consecrated, where sacred symbols may be resuscitated and reilluminated.

Graphic designers often find themselves working on projects that involve worship traditions foreign to them. To fully serve these projects is to understand and respect what is sacred to a particular client and why. What are the differences between designing a book of prayers for a church or designing its letterhead? What if a temple's letterhead conveys a symbol that is considered sacred? How might this inform one's design decisions about ink colors, paper stock, or production methods? Can something be considered sacred-like? Only designers who are able to fully acquaint themselves with the essential sacred elements of a given worship tradition will be able to provide more meaningful and lasting contributions.

In a world obsessed with more, communicators are often challenged by the temptation to fill every square inch of every page with content. Yet many spiritual teachings profess the need for a kind of sacred emptiness, a spiritual state in which room is left for the sacred to inhabit and take root. Emptiness is a concept incongruent with a consumer-based society. Graphic designers wishing to convey a sense of the sacred must trust in the willingness of the viewer to examine their own spiritual conditions and then know when to leave room in their work for such wanderings to take place.

While the intricacies of religion and theology may become tedious or burdensome to a designer on a deadline, the sacred can often be found in the simple and ordinary. As designers strive to grasp a given client's worship tradition, they must learn to recognize the holy in the humble: a simple worship space may be made sacred through a physical gesture of silence; seasonal observances may be marked by the mere change of a color; sacred stories may have a palpable feel to them; architecture, art, or textiles may have a texture or an aura that can be gleaned. All these elements can feed a designer's imagination and inspire new possibilities. But this requires of the designer a mind open to receiving the sacred and an outlook that can be enlivened by the sacred traditions of others.

ISLAMIC CELL PHONE comes with an array of applications that facilitate prayer for thoroughly modern Muslims; a Ramadan calendar, Koranic text in Arabic, and an electronic compass that indicates the direction of Mecca. Model: Ilkone i800.
Photo: Mark Weiss, Smoke and Mirrors Studio

TIBETAN MEDITATION BLANKET embroidered with an endless knot, one of the eight sacred emblems of Buddhism (Fibre Tibet). **CASHMERE THROW** bears the shortened text of a meditation chant (Rubin Museum of Art, NY).
Photo: Mark Weiss, Smoke and Mirrors Studio

METAL BIBLE – THIRSTY? EDITION[†] **Client:** Tyndale House Publishers, Inc. **Agency:** Tyndale House Publishers, Inc.
Art Direction: Barry Smith

ARABIC DISHWARE Client: Baraka **Design:** Tarek Atrissi **Photo:** Mark Weiss, Smoke and Mirrors Studio

Graphic designers wishing to convey a sense of the sacred must trust in the willingness of the viewer to examine their own spiritual conditions and then know when to leave room in their work for such wanderings to take place.

AND GOD SAID LET THE WATERS
UNDER THE HEAVEN BE GATH-
ERED TOGETHER UNTO ONE
PLACE AND LET THE DRY LAND
APPEAR AND IT WAS SO + AND
GOD CALLED THE DRY LAND
EARTH AND THE GATHERING
TOGETHER OF THE WATERS
CALLED HE SEAS AND
GOD SAW THAT
IT WAS
GOOD

GENESIS, 1924 Client: The Nonesuch Press
Agency: Paul Nash **Design:** Rudolf Koch
Illustration: Paul Nash **Photo:** © The Hill Museum &
Manuscript Library, Arca Artium collection, St. John's
University

THE USE OF THE MEANS OF GRACE
Client: Evangelical Lutheran Church in America
Design: Ellen Maly **Cover Cross:** Nicholas Markell

ALL MEN SEEK GOD

CHRISTMAS BOOK: ALL MEN SEEK GOD, 1966 **Client:** North Central Publishing
Design/Illustration: Frank Kacmarcik **Author:** James P. Shannon **Photo:** © The Hill Museum &
Manuscript Library, Arca Artium collection, St. John's University

REVISED COMMON LECTIONARY: PRAYERS AND DAILY READINGS
Client: Fortress Press **Agency:** KantorGroup **Art Direction:** Daniel Kantor **Design:** Jerry Stenback,
Martin Seltz, Becky Lowe

REVISED COMMON LECTIONARY

Prayers

Proposed by the
Consultation on Common Texts

REVISED COMMON LECTIONARY

Daily Readings

Proposed by the
Consultation on Common Texts

The International Design Magazine *God=Details* .... Houston Megachurch .... Laser Buddhas
Jehovah's Contractors .... Modernist Mosque .... Shabbat Technology .... Ideal Meditation Rooms

March/April 2006 / $7.99 US/$11.99 CAN

I.D.

DESIGN AND RELIGION NEW FORMS FOR FAITH

Display Until April 24, 2006

04

0 74808 01511 5

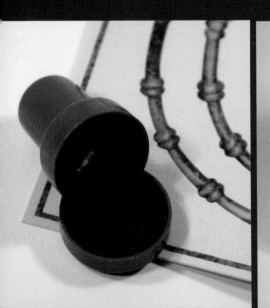

"If liturgy meant literally the work (*ergon*) of the people (*leitos*), then it was not finished until it paid specific attention to where and how that work was completed in the world."[7] It is all too easy, perhaps even lazy, to simply rely upon the sanctity of all things as an excuse not to go deeper, not to work harder at bringing new light to the unseen holy that may be just beneath the surface. To reveal the sacred through art requires effort. It is hard work that requires research, reflection, dialogue, understanding, training, and practice.

7. Lane, *Landscapes of the Sacred*, 182.

Clearly, not all works of art produced in service of religion need be viewed as sacred art. However, it is also reasonable to conclude that something need not be deemed secular just because it is not sacred. It is possible to imbue even non-sacred works with a sense of the sacred. This potential is always present. "The artist should know how to dig out the being that is within matter and be the tool that brings out its cosmic essence into an actual visible essence."[8] Graphic designers today, especially those who work with both religious and non-religious clientele, must be able to recognize the qualities of sacred art that may distinguish it from secular works. Aidan Hart, a distinguished sacred artist, iconographer, and painter tells us that sacred art may be guided by elements that are timeless and boundless:

8. In *Constantin Brancusi* by F. Bach, M. Rowell, and A. Temkin (Philadelphia Museum of Art, 1995), 23.

THE KEY ELEMENTS OF SACRED ART

- Sacred art is humble. Its style leads us beyond itself, albeit through itself, to the divine source of goodness and beauty.

- The artist expresses something of the holy, so the art is not merely the intellectual expression of rational ideas but a description and embodiment of personal experience. And yet it is not self, but God, being expressed.

- Sacred art makes the viewer more perceptive of the God-given spiritual essence of its subject.

- While sacred art reveals the divine, it does not disdain the material expression or "body" through which the divine takes form. It therefore remains incarnate and shows a transfigured world, not a dematerialized one.

- Sacred art often reflects the suffering, hardship, and even apparent ugliness of this life. It is never idealistic or utopian but shares in the reality of our human struggles. It is neither sentimental nor pessimistic.

I.D. MAGAZINE COVER Design: I.D. Magazine **Photography:** Mark Weiss, Smoke and Mirrors Studio

HANUKAH TO GO (with built-in rubber stamp) Design: Luka Ori, Galina Arbeli

- Sacred art does not attempt to isolate the viewer in a purely aesthetic experience. Instead, sacred art makes the viewer more receptive to the sacred as it is revealed. It not only gives us a taste of beauty but aims to make us beautiful.

- Different forms of sacred art are united by universal laws or principles. Because these principles are rooted in the divine, they are not restrictive. They open doors to almost unlimited potential. There is no need to seek novelty at the expense of these principles.

- The individual maker, the artist, is part of a tradition. Therefore, when looking at a sacred work one is not so much aware of an isolated genius, but of an inspired tradition acting through the individual maker or workshop.

- As part of a tradition, sacred art keeps the human person from collapsing into individualism. Each person contributes his or her expression to the tradition; however, the work must remain communal and relational.

- Sacred art not only depicts something sacred, but also, more important, it participates in a sacred process. This process includes the making of the work, the work itself, and the experience people have through the work.

- Sacred art is part of the return of the disordered cosmos to its primal order and beauty.

- Sacred art is part of humankind's expression of worship and thanksgiving to the Creator. It is the using of all one's senses to love God and this world.

- Sacred art is part of the process of discovery, of searching, of inquiry. As a result of this exploration, there is always an element of surprise, youthfulness, and newness to it.

- Sacred art is peaceful and vigorous at the same time. It is peaceful because the artist has cast off egotism and entered the realm of love and harmony. It is vigorous because it attempts to free the viewers' minds and humble their hearts.

- Sacred art is deep. It does not offer platitudes. What makes it sacred is not so much what is depicted but how it is depicted. It is possible both to depict something that is secular in a sacred way and to depict something that is sacred in a secular way.

- Sacred art has an element of imperfection or incompleteness about it. *Imperfect perfection* is something so mathematically or formally complete that there is no room for the viewer. It may be mechanically complete, but it is inorganic. *Perfect imperfection* beckons the viewer to complete the work. It begins a process completed in the heart of the viewer and, therefore, is organic and alive.

- Sacred art has a presence about it. It leads you to the threshold of something. It doesn't violate your free will by whipping up your emotions but quietly leads you to the threshold of another world.

- Sacred art delights in the very medium of which it consists. It does not merely use its medium as though it were a neutral and discardable means to an end. It is the child not only of love between the artist and the subject matter but also of artist and the stuff of the artwork.

- Sacred art's greatness does not reside in quantity but in its quality. It represents something much greater than itself.

- A given sacred artwork does not exist in isolation but is part of a hierarchy; it exists only in relationship with something greater than itself.

- Sacred art is always abstract in the sense that it draws out the invisible essence of its subject. It uses abstractions of style to suggest these invisible realities. It reveals the union of the inner with the outer, the invisible with the visible, eternity in the present.

A more comprehensive listing of the characteristics of sacred art listed above may be found in Aidan Hart's article "The Icon and Art," available through his Web site, www.aidanharticons.com.

(Above) **HAGGADAH FOR PASSOVER, 1965** Client: Trianon Press, Paris Agency/Design/Illustration: Ben Shahn
Copy: Translated with notes by Cecil Roth

(Opposite Page, Top) **CHRISTMAS BOOK: ON THE INCARNATION OF THE LORD, 1961** Client: North Central Publishing Co.
Agency/Design/Illustration: Frank Kacmarcik

(Opposite Page, Middle) **ECCLESIASTES; OR, THE PREACHER, 1934** Client: The Golden Cockerel Press
Design: Eric Gill Illustration: Blair Hughes-Stanton

(Opposite Page, Bottom) **CHRISTMAS BOOK: SEASONS OF HOPE, 1970** Client: North Central Publishing Co.
Agency/Design/Illustration: Frank Kacmarcik Editor/Copy: Sister Mary Alice Muellerleile

Top spread (left page):

If I question Moses as to how it was he saw the burning bush, he will surely reply: Out of curiosity for this strange sight, I approached the spot to take a closer look, but from on high God brought me to a halt. What did he say? Moses, Moses, do not come near. Put off the sandals from your feet, for the place where you stand is holy ground. O what truly divine events! Moses, the servant of God, was not permitted to inspect the spot of the apparition, and yet some of our meddlers vaunt as if they did their prying from some vantage above the Cherubim!

If I question Elias: When you mounted the chariot afire, how, without scorching yourself, could you take in hand and drive horses so fiery and breathing flames? he will surely reply: God gave the command, and the fire was deprived of its native power, Elias was not consumed by contact with fire; neither was the virgin scorched when she received within herself the fire of the divinity.

Top spread (right page):

belly of the whale,... pose a canticle? he will surely reply: He ... second time commanded the whale on my account accomplished this, according to his will, as a type for prefiguring his own burial, and he himself inhabited the tomb and ravished hell of its victims. For God, who is incomprehensible, determines the outcome of events according to his good pleasure.

Middle spread (left book, left page):

THERE IS AN EVIL WHICH I HAVE SEEN under the sun, & it is common among men: a man to whom God hath given riches, wealth, & honour, so that he wanteth nothing for his soul of all that he desireth, yet God giveth him not power to eat thereof, but a stranger eateth it: this is vanity, and it is an evil disease. If a man beget an hundred children, and his soul be not filled with good, and also that he have no burial, I say, that an untimely birth is better than he. For he cometh in with vanity, and departeth in darkness, and his name shall be covered with darkness. Moreover he hath not seen the sun, nor known any thing: this hath more rest than the other. Yea, though he live a thousand years twice told, yet hath he seen no good: do not all go to one place? ✱ All the labour of man is for his mouth, and yet the appetite is not filled. For what hath the wise more than the fool? what hath the poor, that knoweth to walk before the living? Better is the sight of the eyes than the wandering of the desire: this is also vanity and vexation of spirit. That which hath been is named already, and it is known that it is man: neither may he contend with him that is mightier than he. Seeing there be many things that increase vanity, what is man the better? For who knoweth what is good for man in this life, all the days of his vain life which he spendeth as a shadow? for who can tell a man what shall be after him under the sun?

12

Middle spread (left book, right page):

A GOOD NAME IS BETTER THAN PRECIOUS ointment; and the day of death than the day of one's birth. It is better to go to the house of mourning, than to go to the house of feasting: for that is the end of all men; and the living will lay it to his heart. Sorrow is better than laughter: for by the sadness of the countenance the heart is made better. The heart of the wise is in the house of mourning; but the heart of fools is in the house of mirth. It is better to hear the rebuke of the wise, than for a man to hear the song of fools. For as the crackling of thorns under a pot, so is the laughter of the fool: this also is vanity. ✱ Surely oppression maketh a wise man mad; and a gift destroyeth the heart. Better is the end of a thing than the beginning thereof: & the patient in spirit is better than the proud in spirit. Be not hasty in thy spirit to be angry: for anger resteth in the bosom of fools. Say not thou these? For the cause that the former days were better than these? thou dost not inquire wisely concerning this. Wisdom is good with an inheritance: and by it there is profit to them that see the sun. For wisdom is a defence, and money is a defence: but the excellency of knowledge is, that wisdom giveth life to them that have it. Consider the work of God; for who can make that straight, which he hath made

13

Middle spread (right book):

THE WORDS
OF THE PREACHER
THE SON OF DAVID, KING IN JERUSALEM.
Vanity of vanities, saith the Preacher, vanity of vanities; all is vanity. What profit hath a man of all his labour which he

3

Bottom spread (left page):

Hold fast to dreams
For if dreams die
Life is a broken-winged bird
That cannot fly.

Hold fast to dreams
For when dreams go
Life is a barren field
Frozen with snow.

Langston Hughes

Bottom spread (right page):

The last, the very last,
So richly, brightly, dazzlingly yellow.
Perhaps if the sun's tears would sing
against a white stone . . .

As graphic designers embark upon their work within the context of faith, they are encouraged to consider when and if distinctions need to be made between the sacred and the secular. They may even consider that this is not an either/or question but an opportunity to work within a continuum between the two. Many believe that we must strive to create a world that has no need to make such distinctions. Yet until such a world exists, sacred artists are called to challenge and awaken a world that so often fails to recognize the sacred.

Material objects used by many religions are often referred to as *sacramentals*, objects considered to be more than a symbol or a sign, but less than a sacrament. The relative sanctity of any one item is a function of its use, user, origin, meaning, tradition, and purpose. What may be seen as ordinary to one may be holy to another. Designers can play a crucial role in navigating and balancing such distinctions. Critical to this endeavor is understanding what this art form called graphic design is, what it is not, and the specific religious, artistic, and technological values that must shape it.

"Artists, in a way, are religious anyway. They have to be if by religion one means believing that life has some significance and some meaning, which is what I think it has. An artist could not work without believing that."

—Henry Moore, "Primitive Art" from *The Listener* (XXV, 641, April 24, 1941).

THREE STARS CARDS, MARY THE LIVING BIBLE Design/Illustration: Frank Kacmarcik

THREE KINGS CHRISTMAS CARD PANORAMA Design/Illustration: Frank Kacmarcik

Photos: © The Hill Museum & Manuscript Library, Arca Artium collection, St. John's University

MARY
THE LIVING BIBLE

BEARING
THE ETERNAL WORD

WRITTEN
IN HER HEART
AND WOMB

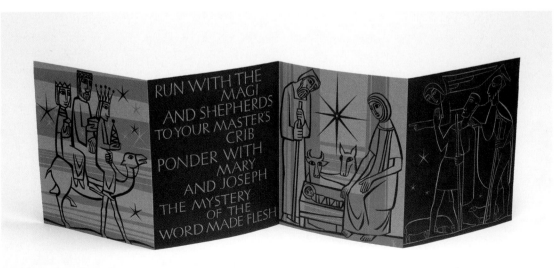

RUN WITH THE
MAGI
AND SHEPHERDS
TO YOUR MASTER'S
CRIB
PONDER WITH
MARY
AND JOSEPH
THE MYSTERY
OF THE
WORD MADE FLESH

DIFFERENCES BETWEEN COMMERCIAL DESIGN
AND DESIGN FOR RELIGION

Commercial design is primarily concerned with explaining and demystifying.
Design for religion must leave room for mystery, often pointing to mysteries without explaining them.

Commercial design often projects illusions through selective or idealized truths.
Design for religion must be concerned with shattering illusions and revealing truths. Design, in the end, is about beauty, which is ultimately about honesty, about God and our response to the divine.

Commercial design prepares the viewer to make purchase decisions that are often concerned with external references.
Design for religion prepares the viewer for prayer, self-discovery, and reflection and encourages the viewer to make internal shifts.

Commercial design rarely speaks to a community but rather focuses on the individual and emphasizes glorification of self.
Design for religion must consider the needs of its community and encourage communal consideration and common beliefs.

Commercial design appropriates symbols and leverages them for their efficiency. They are primarily used as shortcuts to meaning and are often experienced more as signs than as symbols; thus they limit one's vision.
Design for religion must strive to open up symbols and deepen their meaning. A symbol must extend one's vision.

Commercial design is often concerned with speeding up one's decision by attempting to do most or all of the thinking for us.
Design for religion must encourage pause and reflection. It must empower us to think for ourselves and take up our own reflections and decisions.

Commercial design usually employs only what is necessary to achieve its end.
Design for worship is an expression of hospitality, so it must be willing to offer things that may not be necessary or practical.

Commercial design often uses beauty as a façade to enhance perceptions of an offering that may not actually be beautiful or genuine.
Design for religion must offer beauty that originates from the inherent beauty of that which the design serves.

Commercial design is concerned with receiving money, allegiance, loyalty, and attention.
Design for religion must be concerned with giving beauty, truth, mystery, and hospitality.

Commercial design is often concerned with all things new and exciting, trends, styles, fashion, and glamour.
Design for religion must draw upon timeless traditions so as to echo the timelessness of the sacred and divine.

Commercial design often points to an idealized or false reality that may be unattainable, unhealthy, or unnecessary.
Design for religion must be prepared to open our eyes to an authentic reality that is both immanent and transcendent, genuine and attainable.

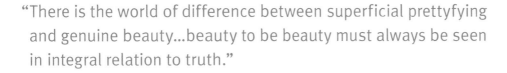

"There is the world of difference between superficial prettyfying and genuine beauty...beauty to be beauty must always be seen in integral relation to truth."

—Richard Harries, *Art and the Beauty of God*, 22.

CHRISTMAS CARD PANORAMA, 1954 Design/Illustration: Frank Kacmarcik

Photo: © The Hill Museum & Manuscript Library, Arca Artium collection, St. John's University

EARTH
FISH
FOUL
BEASTS
HUMAN
CRAFT
& PLAY
MEET
HIM

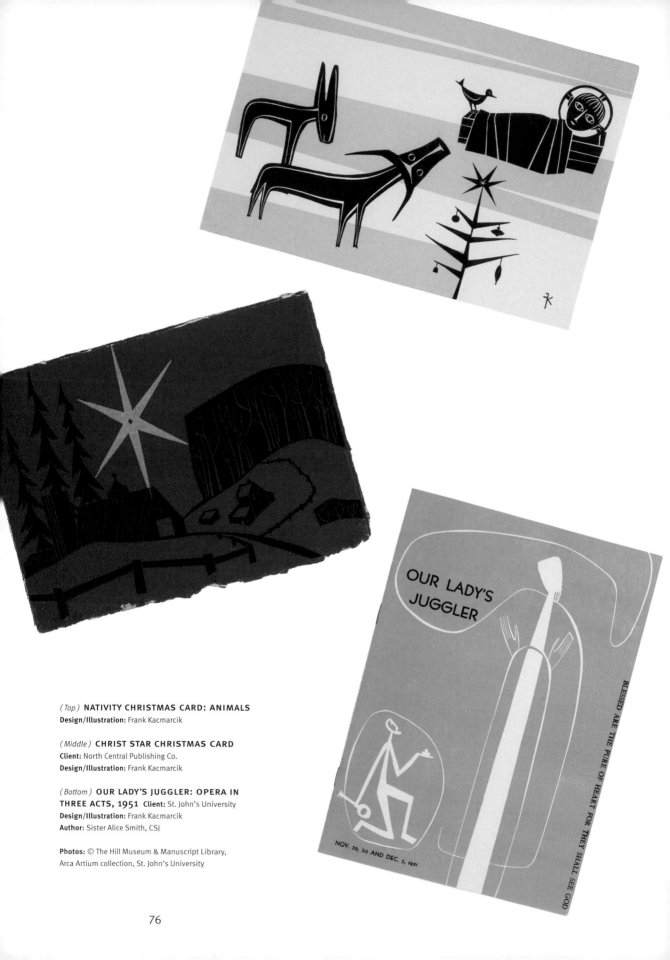

(*Top*) **NATIVITY CHRISTMAS CARD: ANIMALS**
Design/Illustration: Frank Kacmarcik

(*Middle*) **CHRIST STAR CHRISTMAS CARD**
Client: North Central Publishing Co.
Design/Illustration: Frank Kacmarcik

(*Bottom*) **OUR LADY'S JUGGLER: OPERA IN
THREE ACTS, 1951 Client:** St. John's University
Design/Illustration: Frank Kacmarcik
Author: Sister Alice Smith, CSJ

Photos: © The Hill Museum & Manuscript Library,
Arca Artium collection, St. John's University

OUR LADY'S JUGGLER

NOV. 29, 30 AND DEC. 2, 1951

BLESSED ARE THE PURE OF HEART FOR THEY SHALL SEE GOD

(Top) **LECTIONARY FOR MASSES WITH CHILDREN** **Client:** Liturgical Press **Design:** Frank Kacmarcik

(Bottom) **CHRISTMAS BOOKS, 1976, 1970, 1973** **Client:** North Central Publishing Co.
Design/Illustration: Frank Kacmarcik

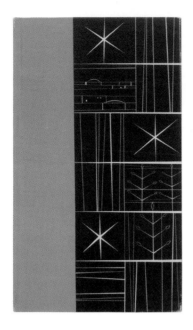

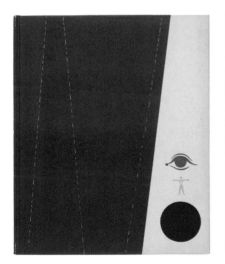
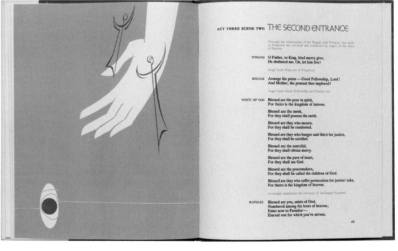

(*This Page, Top*) **A NATIVITY SEQUENCE, 1954** **Client:** North Central Publishing Co. **Illustration:** Frank Kacmarcik **Design:** Jane McCarthy
Copy/Author: John J. Walsh, S.J.

(*This Page, Bottom*) **CHRISTMAS BOOK (A DRAMA), 1957** **Client:** North Central Publishing Co. **Design:** Frank Kacmarcik
Illustration: Brother Placid Stuckenschneider, OSB **Copy/Author(s):** Father Claras Graves, OSB and Cuthbert Soukup, OSB

(*Opposite Page, Top*) **SWEET WAS THE SONG BOOKLET** **Design:** Ben Shahn

(*Opposite Page, Bottom Left*) **CATHEDRAL VILLAGE GREETING CARD** **Client:** Al and Florence Muellerleile **Design:** Frank Kacmarcik

(*Opposite Page, Bottom Right*) **THREE KINGS CHRISTMAS CARD** **Client:** Eloise Spaeth, The Guild Bookshop **Design:** Frank Kacmarcik

Photos: © The Hill Museum & Manuscript Library, Arca Artium collection, St. John's University

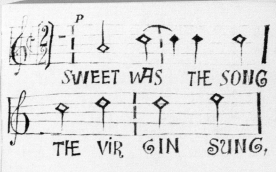

5

The Challenge
of Technology

"Mine is an invitation to rediscover the depth of the spiritual and religious dimension which has been typical of art in its noblest forms in every age. It is with this in mind that I appeal to you, artists of the written and spoken word, of the theatre and music, of the plastic arts and the most recent technologies in the field of communication."

—Pope John Paul II, *Letter to Artists* (Vatican City: Vatican Press, 1999), 34.

IF YOU'VE EVER CHOSEN A TYPEFACE using word processing software, placed clip art in a document, or printed a simple sign or poster, you've made decisions that may seem to fit under the umbrella of graphic design. Yet performing any of these activities doesn't necessarily make you a graphic designer. These are activities more consistent with *desktop publishing.*

A term coined after the introduction of personal computers and printers, *desktop publishing* is more a reference to technology than it is to a medium. Just as knowing how to use a T-square or a power saw doesn't make someone an architect or a carpenter, knowing how to expertly use a word processor or page layout software doesn't make one a graphic designer. Conversely, there are many good designers who know little about the tools of desktop publishing.

Desktop publishing is more concerned with production, convenience, and practicality. It is not, strictly speaking, an aesthetic activity because one needs no aesthetic training or awareness to do it. In fact, those with little or no training are encouraged to do it precisely because the technology is able to do much of the thinking. Using features such as design templates, software filters, plug-ins, and style menus, desktop publishers are able to save time by focusing more on what they do best and less on the demands of aesthetic decision-making.

In comparison, graphic design is an activity that involves years of aesthetic training in the formal elements of art, including "order, unity, variety, contrast, grace, symmetry, asymmetry, rhythm, rhyme, regularity, movement, interval, coherence, dissonance, balance, tension, space, scale, weight, texture, line, mass, shape, light, shade, color, ad infinitum."[9] Certainly, graphic designers are required to become fluent with the tools of their craft, especially computers. But to the experienced graphic designer, the machine is subordinated to the role of aiding in the creation of effective design. Good designers work from the belief that the machine follows and supports the medium. It does not lead.

9. Rand, *From Lascaux to Brooklyn*, 30.

Though many religious organizations have discovered the virtues of desktop publishing technology, it isn't clear that distinctions are being made between desktop publishing and graphic design. Many worship communities are supplied with personal computers, networks, printers, and extensive software libraries, but rarely are these tools chosen for their ability to produce effective, beautiful communications. Within many religious organizations, it is not uncommon to find high-profile communications materials being developed by inexperienced personnel working with inadequate hardware and software, and the results are often less than impressive.

There is an illusion created by many of today's computer tools. Even the most basic word processors today are able to tantalize the user with the promise of endless creativity. The user is rarely required to reflect upon whether a particular aesthetic treatment may be necessary. With a simple click of a mouse button, an unskilled novice is granted access to typeface menus offering thousands of fonts and style treatments. Other visual elements such as colors, lines, textures, and clip art are just a keystroke away. While instruction manuals for software are quick to describe how to use the tools, rarely, if ever, do they educate the user as to why or when to use them. As a result, the discipline of the underlying craft is rarely developed, and one's visual literacy becomes stunted.

WHY
COVENANT
COLLEGE?

VIEWBOOK – COVENANT COLLEGE[‡]
Client: Covenant College   **Agency:** 3HD
Art Direction: Michael Hendrix
Photography: Lane Taylor   **Copy:** Caleb Ludwig

UNI QUE

WWW.

COVENAN

.EDU

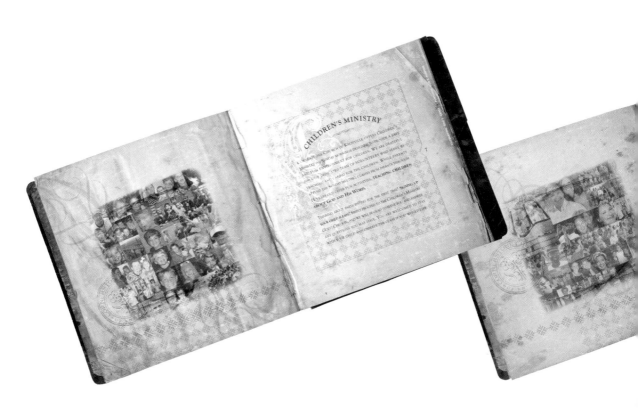

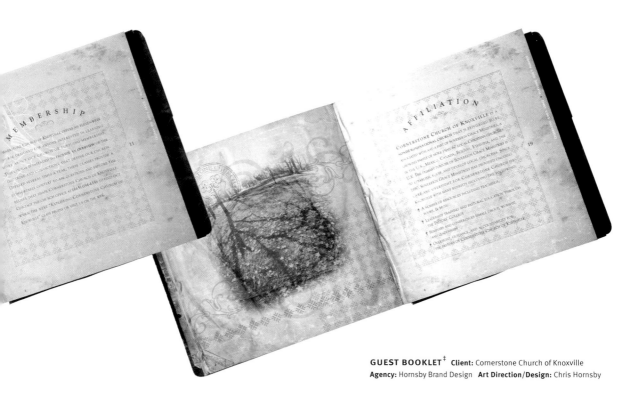

GUEST BOOKLET‡ **Client:** Cornerstone Church of Knoxville
Agency: Hornsby Brand Design   **Art Direction/Design:** Chris Hornsby

85

Consider the following questions:

> What defines identity, and how is consistency maintained?
> What is the underlying concept driving the design?
> What strategic design principles drive the concept?
> How many and which colors should be used?
> How may meaning be assigned to specific colors?
> What are the best ways to communicate through an authentic voice?
> What compositional elements are required to best convey the concept?
> What media types are required? Illustration? Photography?
> What are the best typefaces for a particular project?
> What kind of design grid best serves the project's goals?
> What are the typographic requirements of the project?
> How may content be balanced with space?
> How well will a given design translate to other media?

Only an experienced graphic designer can fully address these questions. Desktop publishing is a tremendous gift of technology, but it presents liabilities worthy of consideration to organizations of faith that so often rely on desktop publishing for its convenience. The more powerful technology becomes, the more the user must be willing to exercise restraint while developing a heightened awareness of the discipline of graphic design. If production is the only concern, the user's works become defined by the limits of the technology and the user's ability to leverage it. Over time, users become dependent upon these limits and are able to visualize only those possibilities within immediate grasp of the technology. This creates a crisis of imagination in which mind becomes lead solely by machine.

The ideal message of faith must convey both a sense of the human and the sacred; it must strive to maintain a connection to the timelessness of its origins and meaning. For even the most experienced graphic designers, this is a daunting challenge. For centuries, the realm of typography, design, and printing belonged only to highly trained professionals who studied and apprenticed many years before they were deemed worthy of their craft. The illuminated manuscripts come from this tradition. Yet in just a few decades, virtually all the tools and awesome responsibilities of the communications design vocation have been made accessible to anyone with a personal computer.

PLTS POCKET FOLDER AND MATERIALS‡ **Client:** Pacific Lutheran Theological Seminary
Art Direction/Design: Annabelle Ison **Copy:** Gaymon Bennett

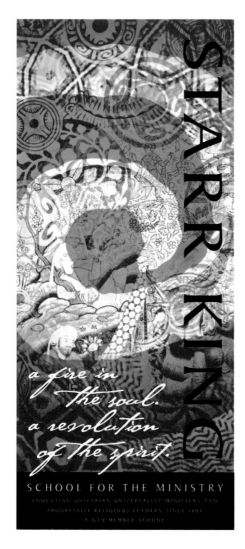

STARR KING SCHOOL FOR THE MINISTRY BROCHURES AND BANNERS ‡
Client: Starr King School for the Ministry   Agency: Kym Thomas Designs   Art Direction/Design/Illustration: Kym Thomas

ARCHEOLOGICAL STUDY BIBLE CONSUMER PROMOTION ‡   Client: Zondervan
Agency: Jager Group   Art Direction: Rob Jackson, Tom Crimp   Photography: Alter Image   Copy: Joy Sarnacke

NEW INTERNATIONAL VERSION

Archaeological
STUDY BIBLE

AN ILLUSTRATED WALK
THROUGH BIBLICAL HISTORY
AND CULTURE

SAMPLER
Genesis 1:1–18:5

❋ First full-color study Bible available,
including over 500 color photographs.

❋ Emphasizes the trustworthiness of the Bible.

❋ Seeks to satisfy a widely-expressed interest in Biblical
archaeology and make the subject accessible to readers.

ZONDERVAN™

NIV
NEW
INTERNATIONAL
VERSION

From the World's Leading Bible Publisher

www.zondervan.com

Most read. Most trusted.

שָׁלַח
מֵאַדְמַת הַקֹּדֶשׁ

(Top) **NEW PROCLAMATION BOOKS** **Client:** Augsburg Fortress **Agency:** KantorGroup **Design:** Kristy Logan

(Bottom, Left) **CIVA HANDBOOK**‡ **Client:** Christians in the Visual Arts (CIVA) **Agency:** World's End Images **Art Direction:** Ned Bustard

(Bottom, Right) **FAITH IS HERE BROCHURE**‡ **Client:** Faith Lutheran Church **Agency:** Bob Heliton Design
Art Direction/Design/Illustration: Bob Heliton

INTERSPIRITUAL CENTRE LOGO, FOLDER, AND WEB SITE ‡ **Client:** InterSpiritual Centre **Agency:** Creative Wonders Communications, Inc.
Art Direction: Diane Lund **Design:** Nancy Page, Dyanne Zircoe

With more and more features being added to newer versions of software, one could spend a lifetime just keeping up with and mastering the potential of a single application. Somewhere, perhaps halfway around the world, a committee is getting together. They're strangers to you, a group of software engineers, marketing managers, executives, salespeople, designers, production artists, and investors who are deciding which features to include in the next version of your page layout software, the very features that may influence the look and feel of your next communications initiative.

It's not hard to lose touch with your humanity, tradition, and authenticity when the communications that express your identity may be produced without your hand ever touching the page, when you need only select a generic software template designed by some distant corporation that knows nothing about you, when the clip art you import is nothing more than a caricature of your spiritual tradition. Much of our contemporary visual experience originates with a machine. It is far too tempting today to substitute the insight of a trained professional with the artificial intelligence of software.

The sheer depth of today's software can be self-serving. A kind of feedback loop is produced in which the software generates new versions that require new training, which leads to further purchases, more training, more updates, more hardware, and, again, more training. Even the most experienced graphic designers find this difficult to manage. Without proper artistic and theological reflection, designers serving religion today can lose touch with the joy and purpose of their efforts.

How can today's designers reinvigorate a soulful connection with the viewer? What is the role of technology in such efforts? Can objects used for worship be deemed sacred if they're produced by hardware and software?

 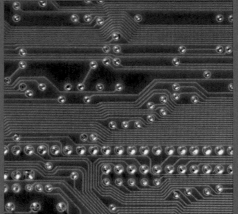 

"It is not technology as such that obstructs and weakens the artist's creative powers, but the circumstance that society fails to control technology and, instead, is controlled by it. Unintelligent use of technology and its products brings an imbalance to the historical life of society and creates a conflict between the living and the dead, progressive and reactionary forces. As a result, centrifugal forces gain strength over forces of cohesion, and man's will to shape the world is paralyzed."

—Paul Rand, *From Lascaux to Brooklyn*, 40.

It is more difficult today to engage oneself in the process of pure making. We're blessed (and perhaps spoiled) by a surfeit of preproduced products and services that require nothing of us with regard to origin or process. Virtually every aspect of modern living involves the use of premanufactured or prepared materials that are the products of technological innovation. These conveniences may be seen as a blessing if they allow us to focus more deeply on our gifts and to catalyze interdependencies that can bring people together and forge relationships. Technology is the means through which we strive to improve our lives and ease life's burdens.

As technology penetrates our lives more deeply, however, we risk losing the ability to be educated by creation. The illuminated traditions teach us that nature can be our teacher. If you don't have a relationship with the materials you use, if you don't love, value, and appreciate the very things that allow you to create, then you can't use these materials to serve as vehicles for the divine. It is not realistic to expect a designer to understand how a laser printer's ink cartridge is manufactured or how the algorithms behind a certain piece of software may work. But it is possible to become more mindful of the stewardship these tools require or to be humbled or even awed by their power. It is possible to raise one's awareness of the effect these tools may have on the environment. It is also possible to innovate newer, more responsible ways through which these tools may be used to illuminate the created world as well as the divine.

"Technologically produced works of art can point toward sacred realities even though they do not possess the more enduring form, color, texture, weight, and density found in more traditional sacred art."

— National Conference of Catholic Bishops, *Built of Living Stones* (U.S. Catholic Conference, 2000), 55.

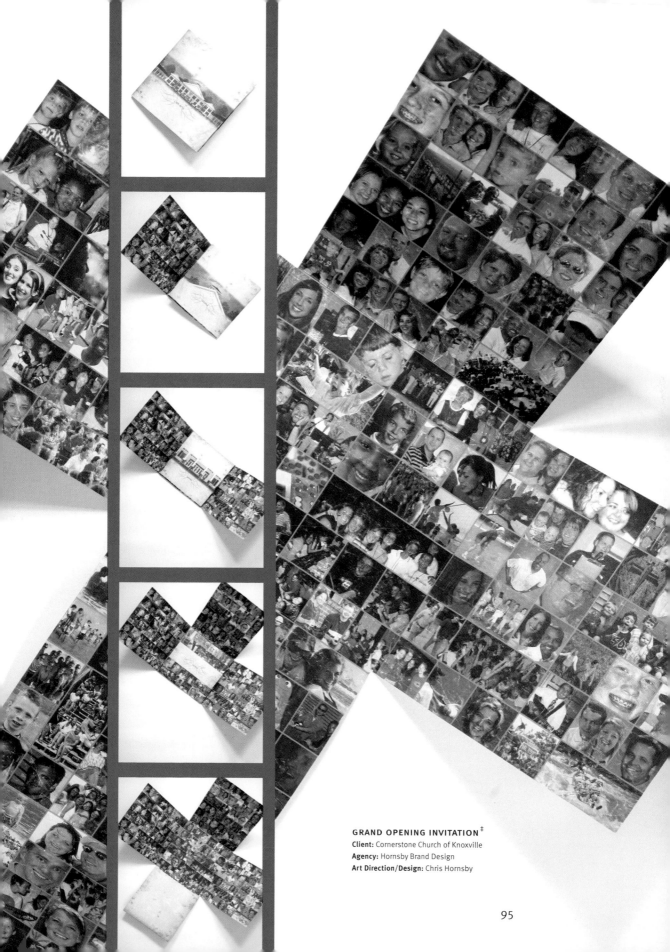

GRAND OPENING INVITATION [‡]
Client: Cornerstone Church of Knoxville
Agency: Hornsby Brand Design
Art Direction/Design: Chris Hornsby

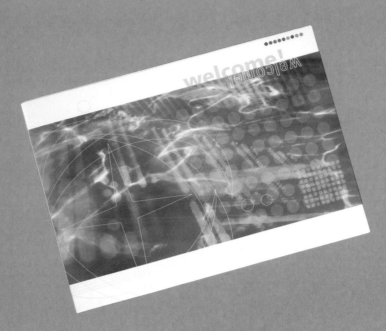

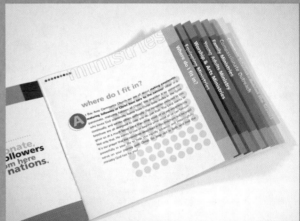

LIFE AT BAY AREA BROCHURES [‡]
Client: Bay Area Community Church
Agency: Exclamation Communications, Inc.
Art Direction/Design: Valerie Cochran

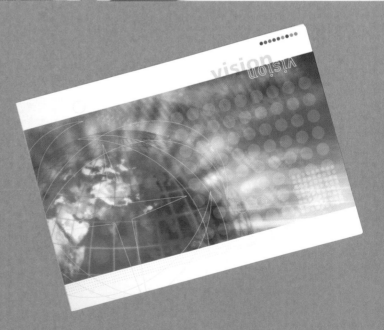

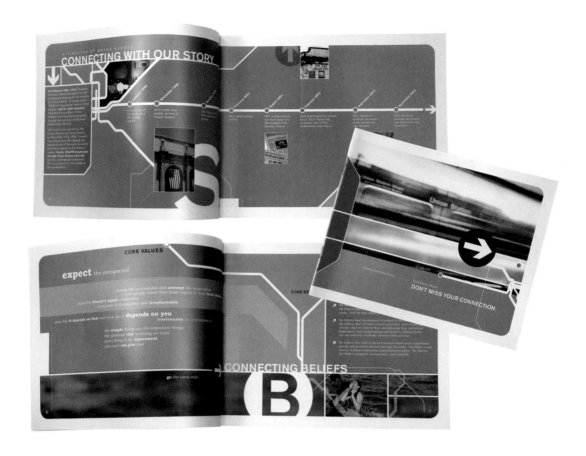

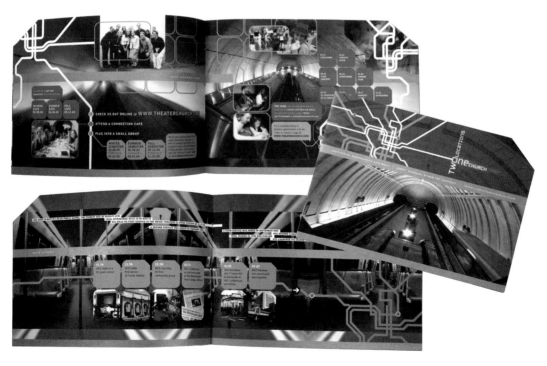

NATIONAL COMMUNITY CHURCH ANNUAL REPORTS ‡ **Client:** National Community Church
Agency: Devotion Media **Art Direction:** Loyd Boldman **Design:** Loyd Boldman, Bryan Kriekard

GCM IDENTITY MATERIALS AND BROCHURE[‡]
Client: Great Commission Ministries (GCM) **Agency:** Devotion Media
Art Direction: Loyd Boldman **Design:** Loyd Boldman, Peter Centofante,
Scott Ahten, John-Erik Moseler

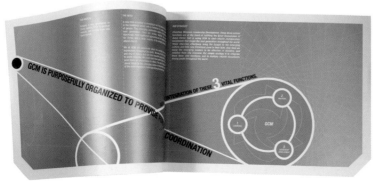

THE ROLE OF CONCEPT AND INTENTION

Computer hardware and software are tremendous gifts when employed properly, but like any tool the technology must be seen as a blessing whose purpose is to give flight to the human spirit of imagination. The best aesthetic concepts must first originate from the mind and be galvanized by a well-developed sense of visual literacy. A beautiful design is not merely an assemblage of visual elements but a unified whole that resonates with the inherent beauty of the human imaginations responsible for it, all of which find their source in the ultimate maker.

Worship environments are filled with sacred objects produced by technology and machine. Even the construction of a sacred space like a synagogue or temple employs serious machinery. The fact that one machine uses software while another uses hydraulics or diesel engines really makes no difference. The capacity of a work to convey either a sense of the human or the sacred has almost nothing to do with the tools employed to create the work. The tools need only be properly guided by a coherent, imaginative concept and the intention to subordinate one's efforts to this concept. Through concept and intention, the vision of a work is made clear and focused.

A concept is the underlying structure of an idea toward which all subsequent development efforts are pointed. It is through the presence of a clear concept that the humanity of any work may be perceived, for a concept cannot be fully conceived without mindful human contribution. Without a concept behind its realization, no work of art is able to convey a clear point of view, which is essential to connecting with the ultimate viewer. The weaker the concept, the less coalescent a work becomes and the more independent its component parts. Under a strong concept, design elements are given a context instantly perceived by the viewer. Component parts become aligned and harmonized, and act as a single unified image. The stronger the concept, the easier it is for the designer to serve the message: the concept becomes the benchmark against which all efforts may be referenced.

To become fully realized, a concept requires clear intention. Without the discipline of intention, the inherent hospitality behind any gesture cannot be fully expressed. Intention is the impetus behind every design decision and the desire to serve the concept to the end. When there is no clear intention behind the component parts of a design, the viewer is instead encouraged to wander. It is conceptual intention that connects viewer with content, content with context, viewer with hospitality, and viewer with the healing power of unity, beauty, and harmony.

"There is nothing worse than a brilliant image of a fuzzy concept."
—Ansel Adams

Let us not become weary in doing

good, for at the proper time

we will reap and harvest if we

do not give up. GALATIANS 6:9

Sowing seeds of hope
Cardinal's Appeal 2003

Sowing seeds of hope
Cardinal's Appeal 2003

Archdiocese of Washington   Winter 2003

Joseph Sherman: A Man with a Mission
By Susan E. Pritchett Post

Joseph S. Sherman, Director of the Sacred Heart Adult
Education Center, is truly a great leader. Despite the
challenges in his life—or maybe because of them—he has
dedicated his life to learning in and service to the Catholic
community.

Sherman's story is one of faith and endurance. Born to a
Muslim mother and a Catholic father, he was raised as a
Catholic in the parish of Sacred Heart in Monrovia, Liberia.
After high school, he worked in the office of an Italian con-
struction company until the Liberian government was over-
thrown in 1980. At that time his supervisor suggested that he
try working for the radio station ELCM, run by the Catholic
Archdiocese.

At the radio station, this self-professed "shy person" found
his voice. He quickly became a popular figure as the
announcer. By revealing and taking a strong
stand against the human rights abuses
of the government, this radio station
was the voice of resistance to the military
government in power. Sherman explains,
"As God-fearing people, we had to speak out,"

continued inside

Archdiocese of Washington ⁄ P.O. Box 98076, Washington, DC 20090-8076 ⁄ (301) 853-4575 ⁄ www.adw.org

ADW CARDINAL'S APPEAL: SOWING SEEDS OF FAITH‡ Client: Archdiocese of Washington
Agency: Graves Fowler Creative **Art Direction:** Theresa Graves, Marianne Seriff **Design:** Victoria Q. Robinson **Illustration:** David Diaz

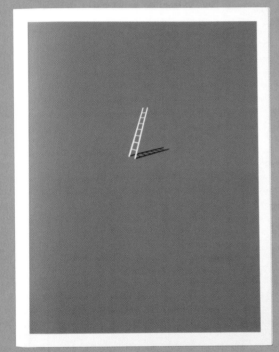

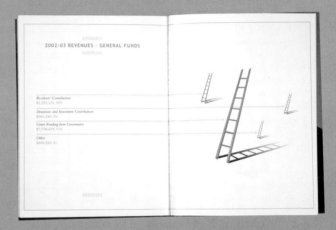

LADDER ANNUAL REPORT ‡ **Client:** LOFT Community Services, Toronto **Agency:** wishart.net **Art Direction/Design:** John VanDuzer
Photography: Michael Hudson, Rev. Jim Lawson, John VanDuzer **Copy:** Rev. Jim Lawson, John VanDuzer

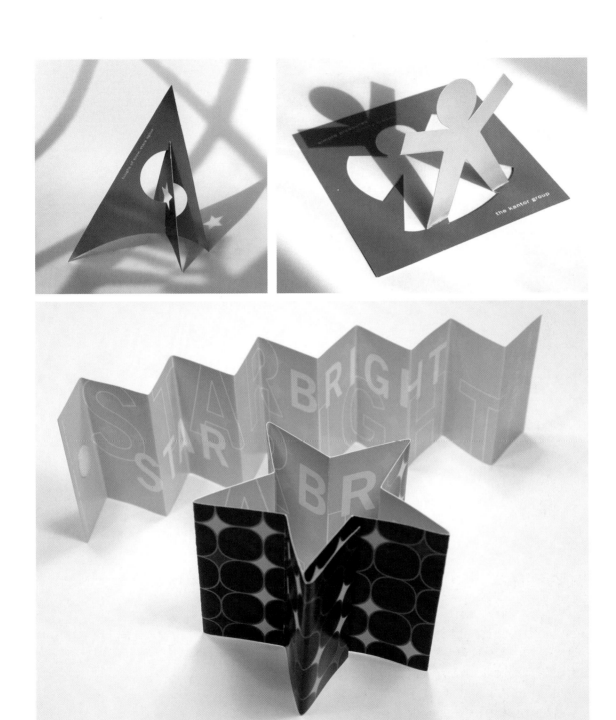

DIMENSIONAL HOLIDAY CARDS **Agency:** KantorGroup **Art Direction:** Daniel Kantor **Design/Copy:** Kristy Logan, Daniel Kantor

"This does not mean that art cannot be mostly for fun — a quick sketch or shriek of delight in life itself. Even this delights the Creator."

—William A. Dyrness, *Visual Faith* (Grand Rapids: Baker Academic, 2001), 101.

ZONDERKIDZ STATIONERY[‡] **Client:** Zonderkidz **Agency:** Jager Group **Art Direction:** Tom Crimp **Design:** Kelli Ruiter

SOUL LIB POSTER 2001[‡] **Client:** Park Avenue United Methodist Church **Agency:** Charles S. Anderson Design Company
Art Direction: Charles S. Anderson **Design/Illustration:** Todd Piper-Hauswirth

july 12th-15th **3400 park avenue**

soul lib

**an outdoor concert
that stirs the soul**
at park avenue methodist church

12th - Soul Lib Choir with Diane White, Larry Long
13th - Cross Movement, Urban Street Level
14th - Excelsior, Groove of Jubal
15th - Salvador • All concerts begin at 6:30 pm.

soul lib 28
SOUL LIBERATION

*If you're feeling lost in an increasingly secular world, please find your way to Metropolitan United Church. With Jesus as your guide you'll never again lose your way. Downtown, Queen & Church Streets * Sundays at 11am*

Seek, and ye shall find.

SEEK AND YE SHALL FIND NEWSPAPER AD[‡] **Client:** Church Ad Project, US   **Agency:** wishart.net   **Art Direction/Design:** John VanDuzer   **Copy:** John VanDuzer   **Illustration:** Derrick Wilson

Join us as we journey together through the highs and lows of Easter.

GO TO HELL NEWSPAPER AD[‡] **Client:** Church Ad Project, US **Agency:** wishart.net **Art Direction/Design/Copy:** John VanDuzer

SEE NO EVIL BROCHURE[‡] **Client:** Mount Oak Fellowship Church **Agency:** Exclamation Communications, Inc.
Art Direction: Valerie Cochran **Design:** Colin Day **Copy:** Colin Day and client

107

1

2

3

4

(All) **POSTERS** Art Direction/Design: Reza Abedini

1. MOHARAM Client: Cultural heritage organization Description:
Poster for an important historical/religious event for Shiite Muslims.

2. & 3. MOWLAVI Client: Mark Bloch University, France Description:
Posters for a ceremony in respect of the great Iranian poet and gnostic "Rumi,
Molana Jalal Al-Din Mulawi" in France. In his rule of life, there is a special form
of dance and rapture, "Sama," which is famous worldwide.

4. CHRISTIAN ART AND PHILOSOPHY Client: Tehran Museum of
Contemporary Arts Description: Speeches on Christian art and philosophy.

**5. AN INTERNATIONAL CONFERENCE ON PHILOSOPHY OF
ART** Client: Tehran Museum of Contemporary Arts Description: Congress for
paintings in the Islamic world.

**6. THE FIRST INTERNATIONAL PAINTING BIENNIAL OF
THE ISLAMIC WORLD CONFERENCE** Client: Tehran Museum of
Contemporary Arts

7. QURAN ON THE MIRROR OF ART Client: Deputy of affairs ministry
of culture and Islamic guidance Description: Poster for the Quran Exhibition,
an exhibition from the historical and ancient Qurans written in different
calligraphy styles, as well as the newly published Qurans.

5

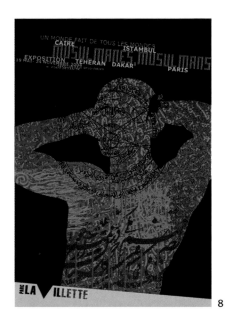

8

6

9

7

8. MUSULMANES, MUSULMANS Client: Parc de La Villette, France
Description: Muslim men and women in five great capitals in the world, a photo exhibition of Muslims in France.

9. THE SECOND INTERNATIONAL PAINTING BIENNIAL OF THE ISLAMIC WORLD CONFERENCE Client: Tehran Museum of Contemporary Arts

Consider the concept of a Zen garden, which is to encourage tranquility and contemplation. Though organic in nature, a closer look at a Zen garden reveals this intention at every glance. No plant, stone, or object is left to chance: the curve of a stream, the placement of a lantern, the rhythm and composition of stones, the color and height of an iris flower, the scale of a cherry tree, and the texture of tall grasses serve a deliberate, intended purpose. All are participants in a form of elemental beauty that brings focus to the mind while engaging the senses with a feeling of completeness. One's outer eye may see the pine tree, but it is the inner eye that experiences its intention.

From bulldozers to sprinkler systems, significant technology may be employed to produce a Zen garden, but the technology is subordinated through concept and intention. Sacred, spiritual, or soulful items can indeed be created using computers, software, and technology. For graphic designers serving religion, technology need only serve the intent of concepts that originate from a human imagination aflame with grace.

Calming one's mind, focusing the senses, trusting imagination, opening oneself up to an ever-present God—these are practices virtually any graphic designer wishing to bring depth and meaning to his or her concepts may embrace. A graphic designer is asked to make hundreds of choices on any given project. The computer must not make all these choices. Like the sustenance of a healthy gourmet meal, it is the vitality and freshness of the ingredients that determine the quality of the end result. Design ultimately entails the responsibility of making choices through intention: it is the choosing of a mystical illustration over empty clip art, deciding to research new typefaces or collaborate with a typographer, selecting photography that is fresh and artful, and hiring a copywriter to craft text that elevates and opens up meaning.

The extensive use of graphic design in religion is reason enough for each faith tradition to more deeply reflect upon how to bring meaning and action into union through message, image, and word. Through concept and intention the integrity of these raw materials is established, and the computer becomes a gift through which these fertile elements are able to gather, take root, and blossom with startling dignity.

111

Graphic Design
A Closer Look

FROM ARCHITECTURE TO MUSIC, art is a familiar, easy-to-identify component of many worship experiences. When you enter a church, mosque, synagogue, or temple you may experience a heightened sense of place, an awareness through which all the senses may be engaged. Perhaps the stained glass windows speak to you, or maybe you're soothed by the sound of a piano or pipe organ or captivated by decorative lettering and ornamentation. When you encounter the mystical beauty of an icon, or the sculptural qualities of an altar or ambo, the effect is just as immediate and inviting.

Graphic design, however, is a bit stealthier—a medium permeating our lives with such penetration that we often fail to recognize its presence. It is the medium behind such things as signs and advertisements, bulletins and hymnals. It is the workhorse art form behind day-to-day communications like business cards, high-volume printed materials, pocket folders, and Web sites. In the secular world, one can't begin a day without encountering commercial logos and branded messages on everything from toothpaste to breakfast cereal. Virtually everything we wear, eat, read, or use is packaged or branded in some way through graphic design. Like it or not, graphic design shapes much of our visual experience and will continue to do so.

At its best, graphic design has the power to "set a mood, generate tensions, surprise, or calm; it can startle or seduce…like music, or like smell, the visual signals shoot straight to the emotions. That is the power of graphics. Language, although immensely powerful,

10. Malcolm Grear, *Inside/ Outside* (New York: Van Nostrand Reinhold, 1993), ii.

seems less immediate, less swiftly channeled into the emotional regions of our minds." [10] Done poorly, graphic design can call attention to itself while obscuring the intended meaning. It can distract, disrupt, or trivialize the content. Worse, it may simply encourage filtering and not be viewed at all.

To design one's messages with integrity is an act of visual hospitality: it is to communicate with a spirit of generosity and clarity. Good design offers the viewer a glimpse of beauty in a world quickly becoming less beautiful. In a commercialized culture of conditional promises and empty rhetoric, graphic design is a medium that represents to religions the opportunity to offer content that gives more than it takes. Even the shortest message asks something of the viewer. What is the viewer to receive in return for their time, attention, and consideration? How can the medium of graphic design be used to enhance this experience?

Although lines have been drawn between *graphic design* and *commercial art* or *advertising art,* such distinctions can mask the obvious: all are concerned with wrapping content in form to suit a particular purpose. While commercial works are concerned with selling — as they should be — the medium of design may be put to use in such a way that the viewer need not feel seduced or coerced. Graphic design at its best can project a message of honesty and openness. It is an art form that represents endless opportunities for responsible faith-based organizations to contrast with a media-saturated, conditional world. Sadly, the vacuum created by the neglect of an art form that has the power to challenge and awaken, to calm and unify, is often filled, instead, by callow substitutes for good design.

Graphic design at its best can project a message of honesty and openness.

ENDOWED BY THE GENEROUS – ANNUAL REPORT‡ **Client:** The United Church of Canada Foundation
Agency: wishart.net **Art Direction/Design:** John VanDuzer **Photography:** Gary Fisher and stock **Copy:** Janet Gadeski
Illustration: Jamie Culson

Endowed by the generous
Enduring for generations
Enabling God's mission

DEFINING "GRAPHIC DESIGN"

Proper reflection on the role of graphic design in religion must include an acknowledgment of the elusive nature of this medium's definition. Each of the words *graphic* and *design* has a broad, subjective meaning and is prone to much personal interpretation. When combined, the two words are no less subjective. For some, *graphic design* is a process or action (a verb) while for others it's an end result, a tangible deliverable (a noun). Some would say graphic design is a profession requiring at least four years of formal study in an accredited school of the arts, followed by a rigorous apprenticeship. Yet it's not uncommon to find people with little or no training claiming the title *graphic designer*. Hundreds, if not thousands of books and periodicals exist on the subject of graphic design, and there are many definitions. The following are just a few examples:

Graphic designer: a professional graphic artist who works with the elements of typography, illustration, photography, and printing to create commercial communications such as brochures, advertising, signage, posters, slide shows, book jackets, and other forms of printed or graphic communications. A visual problem solver.
— *Graphic Artists Guild's Pricing and Ethical Guidelines Handbook*

Graphic design: the art or profession of using design elements (as typography and images) to convey information or create an effect.
— *Merriam Webster's Dictionary*

Graphic (adjective): Clearly outlined or set forth
— *The American Heritage Dictionary*

Design is the fusion of form and content, the realization and unique expression of an idea. Design entails a part-whole relationship expressed in terms of facture, space, contrast, balance, proportion, pattern, repetition, scale, size, shape, color, value, texture, and weight.
— Paul Rand, *Design, Form and Chaos*, 3.

ICHTHUS/FRIEND HALLMARK CARD[‡] **Agency:** Hallmark Cards, Inc. **Art Direction:** Cynthia Bjorn
Design: Brent Morris, Debbie Martin **Copy:** John Peterson, Paige Deruyscher

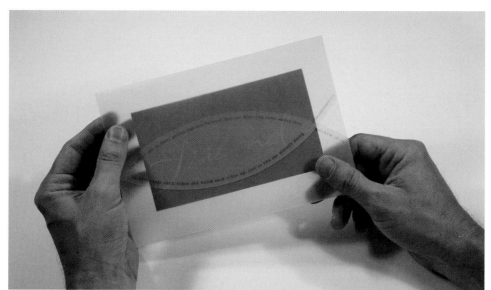

WITNESSING BOOKLET‡
Client: Cornerstone Church of Knoxville
Agency: Hornsby Brand Design
Art Direction/Design: Chris Hornsby

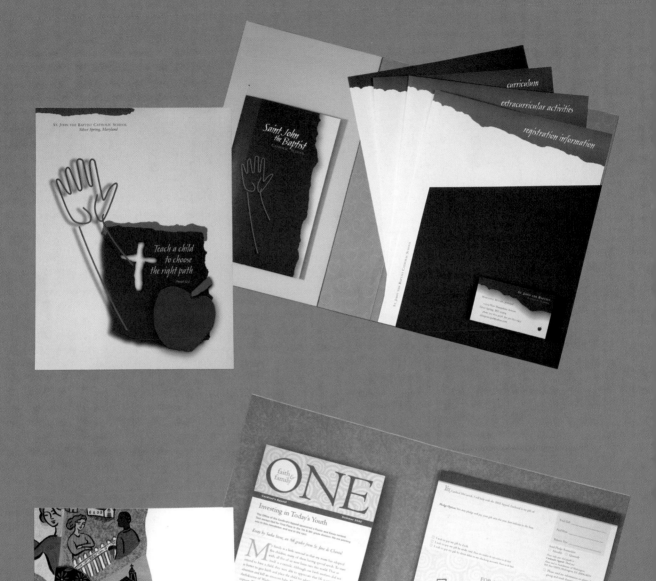

The origins of graphic design as an art form are also often disputed. Some art historians claim graphic design is a focused discipline that began in the early twentieth century when the merging of form and persuasive language found its stride through advertising. Others claim graphic design's origins may be traced to the birth of signs and symbols used in ancient pictographic languages like cuneiform, hieroglyphics, and pictograms. Today most are willing to agree that graphic design is the medium of visual commercial communication. Interpretation of the word *commercial* must be broadened, however, to include the notion of selling or promoting a message or idea rather than just a product or a service, for it would be disingenuous of any faith-based organization to claim they have nothing to promote.

Clearly, religions of the world have a lot to communicate, and graphic design is the medium through which their messages may be clarified and enhanced. Consider the following list of items that a modest-sized place of worship may use to communicate internally and publicly:

Exterior signage	Mailers
Interior signage	Web sites
Directional signage	Member sign-up forms
Event signage	Collection envelopes
Bulletin boards	Hymnals
Kiosks	Lectionaries
Envelopes	Prayer books and ritual aids
E-mail	Service planning brochures
Phone book ads	Diplomas and certificates
Newspaper ads	Clothing, uniforms, and robes
Business cards	Posters
Personal cards	Announcements
Forms, policies, and procedures	Educational aids and resources
Letterhead	Music CDs
Bulletins	Electronic presentations
Name badges and pins	Vestments
Newsletters	Banners and environmental graphics
Calendars	Billboards

LOVE, PEACE T-SHIRT Agency: Sakkal Design Design: Mamoun Sakkal

A+ BILLBOARD – CALVIN CHRISTIAN[†] **Client:** Calvin Christian School Association
Agency: Jager Group **Art Direction:** Tom Crimp **Design:** Andy Filius **Copy:** Joy Sarnacke

THE EPISCOPAL AD PROJECT

In 1979, The Rev. Dr. George H. Martin, an Episcopal pastor in Minneapolis, felt it was time to start reaching people through advertising, a medium that had yet to be used well by churches. For over six years, Dr. Martin worked with Tom McElligott and Nancy Rice of the famed Fallon McElligott Rice agency to produce a series of award-winning ads. The Episcopal Ad Project was so successful the ads were released for use in all denominations.

You shouldn't have to go through channels to talk to God.

He died to take away your sins. Not your mind.

By comparison, any sin you've ever committed is garden variety.

Without God, it's a vicious circle.

There's only one problem with religions that have all the answers. They don't allow questions.

Is the Me Generation doing to Christianity what the lions failed to do?

There's a difference between being baptized and brainwashed.

Now that America is a nation of spectator sports, will spectator religion be next?

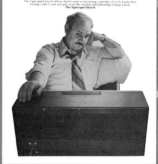

Where women stand in our church.

Will man destroy in six minutes what it took God six days to create?

What other meal can sustain you for a week?

If you think being a Christian is inconvenient today, just look back 1500 years.

Whose birthday is it, anyway?

We believe the important news at Christmas is not who comes down the chimney, but who came down from heaven. We invite you to come and join us as we celebrate the birth of Jesus Christ.

God didn't give His only begotten Son to be a spokesman for the moral majority.

If you think Jesus loves all people — even those who don't agree with Him — come and join us in a service where diversity is our only allowed, but welcomed.

The Episcopal Church

If Jesus fed the multitudes with five loaves and two fishes, why can't the government do it with $800 billion?

If you think it's right to help people in distress, come and join us in an atmosphere where compassion toward people and the worship of God come together in joy and fellowship.

The Episcopal Church

Announcing a religious experience without hallucinations, dizziness or slurred speech.

If you'd like to experience a worship service where trance and emotion come together in a beautiful, sermon-filled tradition, come and join us in the Episcopal Church.

Did Jesus Christ survive crucifixion only to be nailed by Nielsen ratings?

If you find it hard to make a religious commitment to a priest's table, come and join us in worship and fellowship this Sunday. Just live from the Episcopal Church.

The Episcopal Church

Would you read it if the author showed up on the Johnny Carson Show?

The Episcopal Church believes the Bible is more than a gripping fad. We invite you to come and join us as we read from the greatest story ever told each Sunday.

The Episcopal Church

Does Easter mean beans to your kids?

If you agree that Easter should do more for your children than rot their blood sugar level, we invite you and your family to experience the true miracle of Easter in our church.

With all due regard to TV Christianity, have you ever seen a Sony that gives Holy Communion?

If TV Christianity makes you want to switch channels come and join us this Sunday in Christian fellowship and worship without commercial interruption. **The Episcopal Church**

Are your kids learning about the power of the cross on the late, late show?

With all due regard to Hollywood, there's more to Christianity than weeping vampire craft. Come and join us in an atmosphere where our children can learn about the power of the cross this Sunday as we celebrate the resurrection of Jesus Christ in love and fellowship.

The way some churches act these days, you'd think Jesus Christ was an accountant.

The Episcopal Church believes that money is one way to show your faith, but not the only way. Come and join us in an atmosphere where faith comes before finances.

The Episcopal Church

Now that your kids can name the nine reindeer shouldn't they be able to name the twelve apostles?

To help your children discover some of the most unforgettable characters they'll learn today, join us at The Episcopal Church each Sunday as we read from the greatest story ever told.

The Episcopal Church

If all you want from church is hell, fire and brimstone, burn this ad.

Hell, fire and brimstone you won't find at the Episcopal Church. But if it's more exhilarating are the hope of a forgiving and understanding God you seek, join us in worship this Sunday.

The Episcopal Church

The Episcopal Church welcomes you. Regardless of race, creed, color or the number of times you've been born.

Why do you were or have been once or born again, the Episcopal Church invites you and join us in the fellowship and worship of Jesus Christ.

The Episcopal Church

Considering the fact that Jesus had his doubts, why can't you?

If you believe in God, but still have doubts and questions, there's plenty of room for you in the faith and fellowship of the Episcopal Church.

The Episcopal Church

"You can use contemporary language to communicate about God."

—The Rev. George H. Martin

MCCORMICK THEOLOGICAL SEMINARY SIGNAGE **Client:** McCormick Theological Seminary **Agency:** Forcade Associates, Inc.

GIVE YOUR GIFTS CDS **Client:** GIA Publications **Agency:** KantorGroup **Art Direction:** Daniel Kantor **Design:** Jennifer Spong **Illustration:** Katherine Dunn

SWEET MANNA CD **Client:** GIA Publications **Agency:** KantorGroup **Design:** Daniel Kantor **Illustration:** Brian Jensen

WWW.LHBUSTRIP.COM ‡ **Client:** Living Hope **Agency:** Exclamation Communications, Inc. **Art Direction:** Valerie Cochran **Design:** David Wennemar

LUV TICKET *and* **A VALENTINE'S SPECIAL INVITATION** ‡ **Client:** IFGF GISI San Francisco **Agency/Art Direction/Design:** Aryani Kariono

Virtually all of the communications media used by religious organizations may be enhanced or unified under the strategic guidance of a professional graphic designer. Many religious messages are experienced outside of the church and serve as initial points of contact for the viewer. Graphic design is most likely the first medium, and sometimes the only medium, through which members and nonmembers may be introduced to an organization, especially religious organizations. Graphic design is an organization's handshake with the rest of the world and often the point of first impression.

Under a strategic design program, even a simple item like a newspaper ad or poster can become an ambassador, an extension of a unified whole that speaks through a coherent, authentic voice. Without a unifying strategy, which must include aesthetic standards, each of these items will speak through a different voice, project different values, and imply different tastes and styles. This inconsistency encourages the viewer to reidentify with the organization with each encounter. It can signify internal disorder, a failure of coming together. Poorly orchestrated communication is disrespectful of the ultimate viewers and the time they are willing to give in consideration of an organization's messages. The resulting incoherence that may occur over months, years, and decades can culminate in a corrosive effect on perceptions and loyalties.

The question for contemporary religion is not whether to mimic commercial brand sensibilities or, conversely, how to avoid graphic design altogether. The challenge is to define the ways through which religion may leverage this art form's power to enliven and enrich its messages, to reveal its truths through fresh new light. Each faith-based organization or institution is called to reimagine its own visual vernacular in a way consistent with the mystical beauty and grandeur of its core truths, history, tradition, and authenticity. The medium of graphic design can be a powerful strategic tool in these efforts.

For hundreds of years, religions have struggled with the role of imagery versus the role of the written word. Debates on this subject continue to evolve as human innovations in communication continue. Our ability to gain knowledge through the written word has become so sophisticated that it may be all too tempting to dismiss the power of the image to convey meaning. As a result, our ability to see intelligently and experience meaning through the sublime depth of an image may become stunted. Yet there are also many who are unable to read or who would rather not have to read. While literacy rates plummet and information overload increases, it is predicted that future generations may consider

NATIVITY LOGOS AND GRAPHIC STANDARDS MANUAL[‡] **Client:** Nativity of Our Lord Catholic Church, St. Paul, MN
Agency: Ignite **Design:** Jerry Stenback

NATIVITY OF OUR LORD
CATHOLIC CHURCH

NATIVITY OF OUR LORD
CATHOLIC CHURCH

NATIVITY OF OUR LORD
CATHOLIC SCHOOL

NATIVITY OF OUR LORD
EARLY LEARNING
CENTER

written language obsolete, replaced instead by signs, colors, shapes, and audio media that are able to convey information with more efficiency and universality. While image versus text debates are likely to continue, graphic design is the medium through which these two worlds are able to come together today. It is a medium that leverages the strengths of both worlds without placing one above the other.

WHO DOES WHAT?

Graphic design is the art form behind any number of communication specialties and subspecialities. Determining the best design consultant to work with can be a challenging and time-consuming process. Do you need a production artist or a graphic designer? Do you need a design firm or an advertising agency? What's the difference between a marketing communications consultant and a brand consultant?

Within the profession of graphic design there are many titles claimed by its practitioners. Understanding these roles is essential for anyone working within the medium of graphic design. Without consensus, one person's graphic designer may be another person's desktop publisher. If graphic design is to be named as an essential art form for faith organizations, the art form's ambiguities must be addressed if meaningful dialogue is to take place. The following paragraphs describe a sampling of some common titles used within the graphic design profession.

Graphic artist: This title should only be used to describe the broad general category of anyone who works with communication visuals of any kind. It is a very vague term that encompasses all graphic media, such as neon signs, screen printing, sign painting, desktop publishing, graphic design, photography, drawing, illustration, digital imaging, etc.

Anyone who claims to be a graphic artist may indeed be doing specific work, but the title may also be used in a general sense for the purposes of casting a wider net. Similarly broad titles within faith-based professions are not uncommon, including *religious artist* or *liturgical artist.* When artists claim a broad title, they must be encouraged to elaborate on what it means. What media are they experienced in? Where do their skills leave off? Just as a musician can't be skilled on every instrument, a graphic artist is rarely skilled in more than a few media. Most media take a lifetime to master.

Graphic designer: Compared to the title *graphic artist,* the title *graphic designer* is a more specific one used to describe a graphic artist who works primarily with typography, photography, and illustration to produce print communications and/or electronic media.

Edward Eicker

To the Point

Short Chorale Preludes for Organ

MUSIC BOOK COVERS **Client:** Augsburg Fortress **Agency/Art Direction:** KantorGroup **Design:** Jerry Stenback **Illustration:** Nicholas Markell

In contrast with *desktop publishers* or *production artists*, professional graphic designers are often required by employers to have attended an accredited school of art (ideally for at least four years), and to have studied subjects such as composition, typography, communications theory, aesthetics, writing, graphic art history, psychology, sociology, business, and print media production. There are also several postgraduate programs in graphic design.

Because graphic designers find themselves serving a broad range of clientele, any good designer would benefit from a liberal arts education. There are many technical and vocational schools that offer programs in graphic design; however, they tend to emphasize a student's technical and production skills rather than their strategic, aesthetic, or conceptual skills, which take many more years to hone. Depending on the experience level of a particular designer, titles may also include the word *senior, associate,* or *junior.*

Graphic design, like other professions, is parsed into specialties and subspecialties. Some graphic design specialties include print, packaging, interactive media, and books. Some specialize in industries such as food, medicine, banking, or retail. There is a reason specialties exist. Specialists are expected to know more about something, which usually translates to a more meaningful solution.

Art director: Anyone who has a supervisory role in the direction of a graphic design project may assume this title. They may be responsible for choosing talent, such as the designers, copywriters, or photographers on a project. They may also be responsible for selecting illustrations, photography, and other media to be used. Art directors have extensive design experience and are usually graphic designers themselves. In smaller agencies, or when working with freelancers, it is common for the graphic designer on a project to also assume the role of art director. The art director is also sometimes referred to as the *design director.*

Creative director: This is the title used by the person who is responsible for the overall design direction of a firm or an agency. Within the design profession, the person with this title often assumes higher authority than the art director and is required to have many years of design and art direction experience.

Production artist: This title is used by one who is primarily responsible for taking an existing design through the processes required to bring it to completion, from digital file assembly to printing or publishing. A production artist is to a graphic designer what a carpenter is to an architect. He or she builds what has already been designed. Production artists are highly skilled and are invaluable resources to the graphic designer. Many have design skills but prefer to focus on the skillful interpretation of existing designs. As specialists, production artists usually know more than other graphic artists about the technical underpinnings of layout software, prepress techniques, and production issues.

Desktop publisher: This is a title that may be used to describe anyone who has access to a computer that includes simple to advanced publishing software, such as a word processor or page layout application. Desktop publishing is a term that was coined after the introduction of personal computers and printers. Desktop publishers need no formal training in anything beyond the software they use. Knowledge may be gained through hands-on experience or by simply reading a software manual. Some are highly competent while others are not. The presence of a computer on one's desk does not make one a graphic designer or a desktop publisher. It is the nature of the work performed with the tool that creates this distinction.

Freelancers: Though graphic artists are often employed by agencies, many work as freelancers. One of the perceived benefits of working with freelance graphic artists is that they tend to be less expensive. However, the scope of a particular project must be considered when choosing between an individual freelancer and an agency. Freelance graphic designers, for example, may not always be equipped to handle the logistics of a large initiative. The demands placed on a single designer during complex projects can be overwhelming.

Experienced freelancers can provide the benefit of scalability by drawing from a strong network of resources when needed. This is an essential capability that must be assessed when meeting with any graphic designer because even the redesign of a small identity system may require dozens of meetings, prototypes, and reworks. A simple project can generate hundreds of digital files, each of which must be documented, distributed, organized, and archived, and supervising the production of printed materials, from business cards to envelopes, can involve dozens of print estimates and demanding production schedules. The best of intentions are easily humbled by the rigors of a complex communications design project. The best freelancers are honest about their capabilities and know when to bring in additional support as necessary.

FIRMS AND AGENCIES

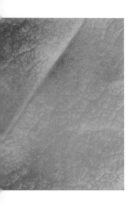

Creative firms that provide graphic design services also take many forms. Twenty years ago there were clear differences between advertising agencies and design firms. In today's brand-centric multimedia world there is more ambiguity between the types of organizations that provide graphic design. Generally speaking, creative firms may be described as follows:

Graphic design firms: any firm that uses the word "design" to describe itself will place a high value on form, concept, and aesthetics. Graphic design firms tend to offer communications and packaging design solutions for a broad range of media. They tend not to emphasize any one communications vehicle (the way an advertising-oriented agency might). Instead, the focus is first placed on the integrity of the design solution. Graphic design firms tend to be smaller, so they typically offer the advantage of lower overhead and quicker response times. However, they may not have the broad range of internal resources a larger agency may have, so on logistically challenging projects they may actually require more time, which can increase costs.

Advertising agencies: Although use of the term *advertising agency* is still frequent outside the creative industry, this nomenclature is quickly becoming a thing of the past within the creative profession. Since most agencies provide services that extend far beyond advertising, the term *advertising agency* may be too limiting. Most of the former advertising agencies now do business as *brand strategy firms* or *marketing communications agencies*, or simply *creative agencies*. Today's version of the big advertising agency tends to service larger national accounts and is up to accommodating simple to complex national and international media campaigns, including print, TV, radio, Web, packaging, and direct-mail advertising. The level to which advertising agencies are able to focus on good design varies greatly. And just as there are large and small graphic design firms, the same is true for ad agencies.

Marketing communications firms: This is another term that was coined to describe any firm not wanting to be niched as a pure ad agency. Until branding became the focal point of most creative agencies, *marketing communications* was used to describe the broad range of communications tools required to market a product or service. Some firms still use this term; however, many now use *brand communications* instead. *Marketing communications* is also the generic term used to name the broad category that most creative firms operate within.

Public relations firms: Also referred to as *PR firms*, these are agencies that help clients optimize how they are publicly perceived. They are especially qualified to help organizations tell their stories, control media perceptions, and generate editorial coverage in magazines, newspapers, television, and other mass media. Like advertising agencies, some public relations firms have broadened their services to include broader marketing communications efforts, like brand consulting, advertising, and graphic design. In fact, most PR firms' descriptions of themselves sound a lot like those of other creative agencies.

Web and interactive developers: Since the introduction of the Internet, every creative agency has struggled at some point with how to provide services pertaining to Internet and Web development. There are also many creative firms now that focus solely on these technologies. When working with a dedicated Web developer, consistency must be maintained with other communications media, such as print. This is one of the biggest challenges when working with a Web-only resource. They may not have the intimacy or client history required to fully integrate with an organization's other media expressions. Cross-media dialogue and integration are essential if an organization's voice is to remain consistent across all forms of its communications.

Faith-based firms: Firms that specialize in faith-based clientele developed many of the works shown in this book. The same agency distinctions listed above may be applied to these specialists. Again, the extent to which any of these firms focuses on design as compared to advertising services, brand consulting, or public relations varies from firm to firm.

Though there are many professional commercial organizations that bring graphic designers together, at the time of this writing there do not appear to be many organizations dedicated to the specialty of religious graphic design or faith-based communication design. The design profession would benefit from such a group, especially if it welcomed designers and communicators from the world's many worship traditions. As demand for this specialty increases, the likelihood of such an organization being formed should increase.

Two organizations that are worth noting include Christians in the Visual Arts (CIVA) and the National Council of Churches Communication Commission, both listed in the *Resources* section of this book.

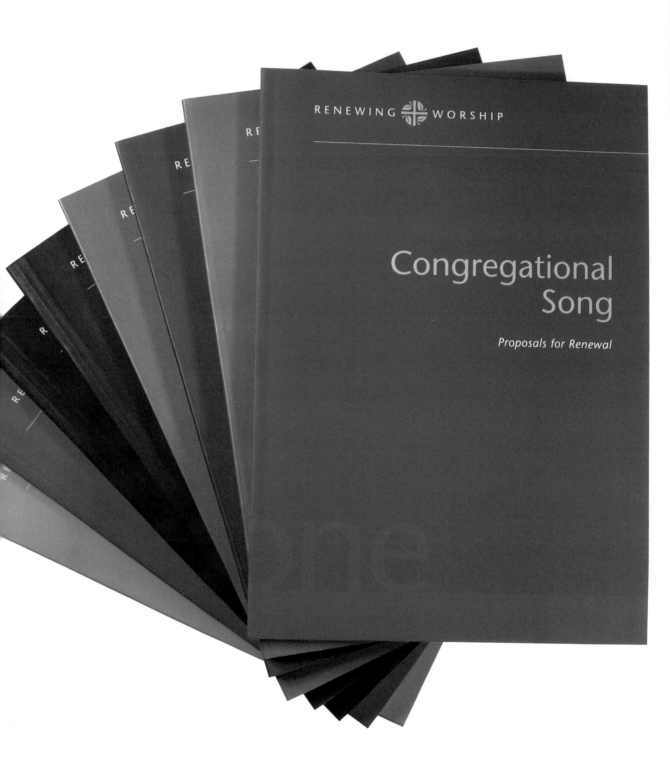

RENEWING WORSHIP **BOOKS 1–8** **Client:** Augsburg Fortress **Agency:** KantorGroup **Design:** Carolyn Porter **Logo Design:** Nicholas Markell

136

Branding agencies: It's hard to find a creative agency today that doesn't claim some form of branding expertise. Branding is the biggest philosophical focal point to hit the creative communications profession since the introduction of the desktop computer. From freelance graphic designers to big agencies, branding is now the ground they all walk on. In fact, any of the agency types discussed up to this point could very well be doing business as a branding firm of some kind.

Some marketing analysts claim branding is a dying discipline to be replaced, instead, by agile communications media better able to adapt to an ever-evolving world of micro-markets. Other analysts assert that a new branding movement has already begun, and it's called *design*. It seems businesses worldwide are discovering what the great American designer Paul Rand said years ago: "Good design is goodwill." Like so many other subjective terms in the field of graphic design, branding is a term that can mean different things to different people.

MORE ON BRANDING

Your webmaster isn't concerned with your letterhead; your banner artist isn't concerned with your signage; and the freelance desktop publisher you retained for your yellow pages ad isn't concerned with your worship programs. A good graphic designer, however, should be concerned with all of these things. Under the direction of a qualified design strategist, each of these seemingly independent expressions of your faith community can be unified through a single voice. These aspects ultimately fall under the category of *branding*.

Branding is a term that refers to the strategic efforts of an organization to unify such things as image, identity, and the emotional experiences one's products or services create for specific customers or audiences. When subordinated to the discipline of branding, graphic design becomes a unifying vehicle for delivering differentiated, memorable messages and experiences that motivate decisions and inspire loyalty. It is the framework through which visual communications become coherent.

There are cynics within faith-based organizations who would rather not use the term *branding* due to its commercial connotations. Whether or not you accept the label *branding,* strategic efforts made to unify the communal voice of any faith-based organization can deliver meaningful benefits. Branding efforts can have the effect of bringing members together, raising necessary and healthy questions, strengthening dialogue, enhancing messages, and clarifying roles within the broader community. Many faith-based organizations would benefit from this strategic approach to their communications efforts. The practice of unifying the totality of a faith-based organization's communications efforts is not a new idea, as described earlier. One could even argue that the idea wasn't invented by business.

Branding initiatives often follow strategic planning efforts. When an organization chooses to map out a new direction, for example, it's not uncommon for such an initiative to inspire the need for a new brand identity system. A refreshed identity system is often required to more accurately reflect the renewed culture of an organization.

The marketing of any organization can be stressful and chaotic. Efforts often involve committees and consultants, all of whom may generate reams of data and information, leading to months of additional analysis and discussion. In the midst of the noise and chaos of such endeavors it is easy to lose sight of one simple fact: the end results of these efforts are usually conveyed through the medium of graphic design. If the end result isn't beautifully relevant, all efforts may be for naught. The efforts of the best committees and brightest consultants may be rendered meaningless without a competent graphic designer to bring it all together through form. In this context, the graphic designer must be seen as a long-term strategic partner.

As organizations become more aware of the volume of their media expressions, as well as the unifying benefits of branding, the need for assigning a brand manager becomes more evident. A brand manager may be the graphic designer or someone within the client organization with experience in supervising the development of communications media. The brand manager's responsibility is to ensure that every relevant communications sightline to an organization is properly aligned and subordinated to a greater whole. The brand manager brings sanity and discipline to what could otherwise become a creative free-for-all.

THE NEED FOR HIGHER STANDARDS

There is a perception that certain fields don't function under ethical guidelines, especially those that have no licensing or accreditation. Because there are so many practitioners and specialties in the design field, graphic designers and the clients who retain them must be held to the same ethical standards as other professionals like lawyers and doctors. The importance of contracts, guidelines, and agreements between designers and their clients has never been higher, and professional practices are critical to the integrity of the profession. Ignorance of the importance of professional standards will inevitably lead to abuses. Graphic design is a widespread medium that is too easily exploited and sold short of its true value. To receive the fullest benefit of this art form, religions may need to define the boundaries and standards of their graphic design practices. Only then will the fullest benefits of design be realized.

(Top) **JAMES RIVER IDENTITY MATERIALS** [‡] **Client:** James River Center for Expository Preaching
Agency: Devotion Media **Art Direction/Copy:** Loyd Boldman **Design:** Peter Centofante

(Bottom) **NAUVOO ILLINOIS TEMPLE PRESS KIT** [‡] **Client:** Temple Department **Agency:** Eric P. Johnsen
Art Direction: Stan Thurman, David Vandivere, Eric Johnson, Scott Mooy **Design:** Paul Killpack, David Vandivere, Lee Workman

Typography
The Power of the Designed Word

GRAPHIC DESIGN IS THE ART FORM that best represents the fusing of words with images and the shaping of words through form. One cannot practice graphic design without learning to master the art of the designed word: *typography.*

Religions of the world have always emphasized the power of the word. Some even emphasize the word over all other human expressions. The written word of the Christian Bible is considered by some to be the primary manifestation of God's presence in this world. Islamic traditions emphasize the power of God's name through beautiful calligraphy and all but eliminate representational imagery. Illuminated text traditions from Judaism, Buddhism, and Hinduism further demonstrate the power of the designed word, for when word takes form through beautiful lettering it becomes a visual celebration of the inherent beauty of the texts' truths.

Typography and the written word have often been driven by religion. The first book to be printed using movable type was the Gutenberg Bible, and its typographic design was influenced by practices of proportion and ratio handed down by the scribes and calligraphers of religious manuscripts. Even today's most familiar typefaces incorporate details derived from calligraphy (e.g., the varied stroke weight of the letter "o"). Religions can take pride in their contributions to typographical developments, for without the zeal to proclaim their messages through written texts, the rich tapestry of typography available to us today would be much different, less rich, and certainly less beautiful. Some of the world's greatest artisans left us with letterforms, typographic tools, and methods that have continued to thrive for centuries. One need only select a typeface like Garamond to participate in this history.

Mastering typography requires as much professional development as any other aspect of design and may take a lifetime to master. For some designers, typography is the only art form they work with. Within the graphic design profession, it is not uncommon for a designer's competence to be measured by how well he or she uses type. The designer who can produce beautiful typography is the designer who is willing and able to pay attention to details. Yet it is also a craft that requires a healthy sense of humility, for typographers might never be noticed or have their skilled efforts appreciated. "In a masterpiece of typography, the artist's signature has been eliminated."[11] Like artists of sacred icons that often bear no artist's name, designers are often unknown to their audience. Yet iconographers are rewarded in the belief that they are instruments for the sake of beauty and that God is the true author of their efforts. Today's designers may find inspiration in such a perspective.

Good typography is the communicator's expression of visual hospitality. The designer must first ensure that texts are legible because, unlike expressive imagery, typography is meant for everyone who can read. It is not just for those who may be artistically literate.

Poor typography can ruin an otherwise beautiful composition. For example, by improperly spacing the letters of a word, the word itself, which is meant to be experienced as a symbolic unit, is seen instead as a grouping of letters stripped of their unification. Reading poorly set type can be a fatiguing experience. The reader need only glance at a paragraph of copy to determine whether it is to be read or filtered, a decision made subconsciously as a function of the typography. "If you start looking closely at the type you see every day, you'll be amazed at the number of typographic improvements that could have been made but weren't. The problems result from various portions of haste, ignorance, greed (managers who won't pay for expertise, training, or quality control), and—saddest of all—a simple lack of concern."[12]

11. Jan Tschihold, *The Form of the Book* (Vancouver: Hartley & Marks, 1997), 4.

12. James Felici, *The Complete Manual of Typography* (Berkeley, CA: Peachpit Press, 2003), 111.

Garamond

In the mid-1500s, Claude Garamond, a French metal punchcutter and type designer, produced a refined family of book typefaces. His designs combined an unprecedented degree of balance and elegance. The typeface *Garamond* is still in widespread use today and stands as a pinnacle of beauty and practicality in typefounding. It is also the typeface used for the body of this book, *Graphic Design and Religion*.

PRIERES PENDANT LA MESSE A L'USAGE DE MADAME LA COMTESSE DE VOISENON (BOOK OF MASS PRAYERS, 1752) Design: Canon Ph. Ch. Gallonde

HEURES NOUVELLES TIRÉES DE LA SAINTE ECRITURE, 1685 Design: Louis Senault

The printed word has often driven technology, and technology has often driven the printed word. Below, hand manuscript imitates set type (top) and set type imitates hand manuscript (bottom).

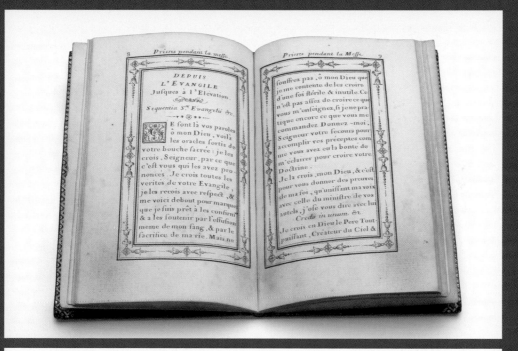

Conversely, when a designer makes text readable, the content of the message is made available to the reader in a way that is virtually irreversible. Good typography facilitates a rapid, precise exchange of ideas and is perhaps one of the most efficient ways to transport information, knowledge, and wisdom that humans have ever devised. When texts are well set, the many individual, disconnected letters and words come together to form a whole that may be experienced through time with little effort, almost like the way we experience music through time.

Scientists have demonstrated that human beings read by the process of recognizing the shaped outline of words. Additional studies suggest that we read by seeing each word as a whole and recognizing each word by its cumulative "look," which is a function of the interrelatedness of letter combinations. A good typographer, then, must appreciate the importance of the visual relationships found in letter combinations and the role they play in word recognition. Type that is easy to read can bring out more of the message's beauty.

In a world that hungers for meaning and substance, beautiful typography presents any religion with the opportunity to mirror and extend the beauty of its messages. Sacred texts that have survived thousands of years need not be decorated or adorned with excessive arbitrary treatments. They need only be honored through the humility of an art form that is able to illuminate without upstaging the message or coercing the reader. The beauty of truth need only be conveyed through letterforms that have been painstakingly designed for us, typefaces that have already stood the test of time.

The timeless messages of religion and faith are often well served by a timeless typeface. Designers today have at their disposal many typefaces that exhibit qualities perfected by centuries of use. Grace, beauty, proportion, and unity are already inherent in any classic typeface. Good typography often involves letting a typeface be what it was meant to be: legible. It means executing fundamentals and getting out of the way, nothing more.

Some scientists refer to the shaped outline of a word as the *bouma shape* in reference to hypotheses developed by the prominent vision researcher H. Bouma.

"It is the supreme duty of responsible designers to divest themselves of all ambition for self-expression. They are not the master of the written word but its humble servants."

—Jan Tschihold, *The Form of the Book: Essays on the Morality of Good Design*, 11.

TRUE IDENTITY BIBLE[‡] **Client:** Livingstone Corporation **Agency:** Spire2 Communications, Inc. **Design:** Jeffery James

⁸It is better to take refuge in
the LORD
than to trust in human
beings.
⁹It is better to take refuge in
the LORD
than to trust in princes.
¹⁰All the nations surrounded
me,
but in the name of the LORD
I cut them down.
¹¹They surrounded me on every
side,
but in the name of the LORD
I cut them down.
¹²They swarmed around me
like bees,
but they were consumed as quickly as burning thorns;
in the name of the LORD I cut them down.
¹³I was pushed back and about to fall,
but the LORD helped me.
¹⁴The LORD is my strength and my defense*;
he has become my salvation.

¹⁵Shouts of joy and victory
resound in the tents of the righteous:
"The LORD's right hand has done mighty things!
¹⁶ The LORD's right hand is lifted high;
the LORD's right hand has done mighty things!"
¹⁷I will not die but live,
and will proclaim what the LORD has done.
¹⁸The LORD has chastened me severely,
but he has not given me over to death.
¹⁹Open for me the gates of the righteous;
I will enter and give thanks to the LORD.
²⁰This is the gate of the LORD
through which the righteous may enter.
²¹I will give you thanks, for you answered me;
you have become my salvation.

²²The stone the builders rejected
has become the cornerstone;
²³the LORD has done this,
and it is marvelous in our eyes.
²⁴The LORD has done it this very day;
let us rejoice today and be glad.
²⁵LORD, save us!
LORD, grant us success!

²⁶Blessed is he who comes in the name of the LORD.
From the house of the LORD we bless you.ᵇ

ᵃ song   ᵇ 26 The Hebrew is plural.

conversations

trust — 118,8-9

1 ⟫ Is it ever safe to completely trust another person?

2 ⟫ Would you describe yourself as a trusting person or not? What's made you this way?

3 ⟫ Does your level of trust in others affect your trust in God?

For more on trust, check the index.
For the next Conversations, go to p. 825

828

²⁷The LORD is God,
and he has made his light shine on us.
With boughs in hand, join in the festal procession
upᵃ to the horns of the altar.
²⁸You are my God, and I will praise you;
you are my God, and I will exalt you.
²⁹Give thanks to the LORD, for he is good;
his love endures forever.

Psalm 119ᵇ
א Aleph

¹Blessed are those whose ways are blameless,
who walk according to the law of the LORD.
²Blessed are those who keep his statutes
and seek him with all their heart—
³they do no wrong
but follow his ways.
⁴You have laid down precepts
that are to be fully obeyed.
⁵Oh, that my ways were steadfast
in obeying your decrees!
⁶Then I would not be put to shame
when I consider all your commands.
⁷I will praise you with an upright heart
as I learn your righteous laws.
⁸I will obey your decrees;
do not utterly forsake me.

ב Beth

⁹How can those who are young keep their way pure?
By living according to your word.
¹⁰I seek you with all my heart;
do not let me stray from your
commands.
¹¹I have hidden your word in my heart
that I might not sin against you.
¹²Praise be to you, LORD;
teach me your decrees.
¹³With my lips I recount
all the laws that come from your
mouth.
¹⁴I rejoice in following your statutes
as one rejoices in great riches.
¹⁵I meditate on your precepts
and consider your ways.
¹⁶I delight in your decrees;
I will not neglect your word.

²⁷ Or Bind the festal sacrifice with ropes / and take it   ᵇ This psalm is an acrostic poem; the verses of each stanza begin with the same letter of the Hebrew alphabet.

829

conversations

purity — 119:9-16

1 ⟫ What does it mean to be pure in our world today?

2 ⟫ In what areas of your life do you have the most difficulty with purity?

3 ⟫ How does God's Word help you remain pure?

For more on purity, check the index.
For the next Conversations, go to p. 841.

true.identity

When a reader views even basic copy, a skillfully typeset word is not experienced as a grouping of letters, but rather as a unified symbol. The reader does not reflect upon the letter spacing or the ascender heights. He or she sees through the letters and words and experiences only meaning. Like the best symbols, good typography transcends and points beyond itself. When texts convey symbolic subject matter—as do so many religious texts—a humble word like "bread" sets off an almost miraculous chain reaction, each layer pointing to the next in an instant cascade of transcendence:

- The grace of the letterforms invites the eye in.
- The letter symbols form a word symbol.
- The word symbol evokes literal meaning.
- The literal meaning points to deeper, broader metaphoric meaning.

Like an invitation to a meal, good typography prepares the written word for a feast of visual consumption that can be most satisfying and enjoyable for the reader.

The joy delivered by typography may be found in its unity and harmony. Through the unity of typography's letters, words, paragraphs, heads, subheads, serifs, dashes, and numbers, a single story may be told. When in harmony, type alone can be beautiful, an image as graceful as any expressive art form. Typography within this context follows the tradition of calligraphy, which translates to "beautiful writing."

PROPORTION AND RATIO

In typography, harmony is often a function of proportion and ratio. Through each, one is able to experience a book, for example, through its physical size and its capacity to accommodate the human hand; through the balance of space and content the eye may enter into the page as if walking into another world. The proportions of a single letter-form are designed to aid the eye in discerning an almost infinite number of variables and relationships. Change just a single detail of one letter in a typeface, and the entire typeface could become useless.

THE ALPHABET OF CREATION: AN ANCIENT LEGEND FROM THE ZOHAR, 1954 **Client:** Pantheon Books
Design/Illustration: Ben Shahn **Photos:** © The Hill Museum & Manuscript Library, Arca Artium collection, St. John's University

Next came Pe that claimed the
word Podeh, the Redeemer, to
his credit. But God said, "You
have the lowered head, symbol of
the sinner who, ashamed, lowers
his head and covers it with his

arm. Besides, Peshah, transgres-
sion, reflects dishonor upon the
letter Pe."

world through Beth; as it is said,
"Bereshith—in the beginning—God
created the Heaven and the Earth."

The letter Aleph remained in her
place. And the Lord, blessed be He,
said to her, "O Aleph, Aleph, why
have you not presented a claim
before Me, as have the other
letters?" Aleph replied, "Master of
the Universe! Seeing that all these

Heth, although it is the first letter
of Hanun, the Gracious One, is also
first in the word for sin—Hattat.
So the letter Heth was rejected.
Zayin based his plea upon the fact
that he begins the verse which

ordains the observance of the
Sabbath. But God said, "You may
not help Me in the work of the
creation of the world, for Zayin
is the word for weapon, which is
the image of war."

The incorporation of proportion into one's artistic works has long been aligned with the belief that such efforts open the door to a deeper perception of the divine as revealed through the proportions found in the created world. It is fitting, perhaps, that typography often draws upon a specific proportional relationship referred to as the *golden section* or *divine proportion*, a compositional tool that has been in use for thousands of years in music, painting, poetry, drawing, and architecture. In the divine proportion, three dissimilar parts of a whole share a same universal ratio of proportion. This ratio represents to some the possibility that behind the chaos of this universe an ordered harmony exists in all things. In this light, the divine proportion is seen as a symbol or signature of God's presence, a certain sacred geometry.

Proportion is rarely concerned with symmetrical perfection. A well-proportioned page of type may have wider margins on one side or may have ragged edges along one side of a paragraph. A perfectly centered title is often best followed by a subhead that's left justified. "Indeed, disturbance of perfect symmetry is one of the prerequisites for beauty. Anything not quite symmetrical is considerably more beautiful than faultless symmetry." [13] Typographic grid designs can embody the same qualities of imperfect symmetry found in the human face, in a tree, or in a piece of fruit. It is through this tension between symmetry and asymmetry, between the similar and dissimilar, that the eye is able to move through a written work. The static nature of perfect symmetry with no tension cannot move us with the same warmth or resonance.

13. Tschihold, 34.

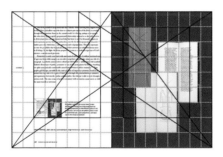

THE GOLDEN SECTION
The golden section is an ancient Greek formula developed by Pythagoras to help understand the beautiful proportions so often found in nature. In art, architecture, and science, the golden section is used to create balanced, classic proportions—principles used in the design of this book.

NATIVITY KERYGMA, 1958 Client: North Central Publishing Co. **Design:** Frank Kacmarcik **Author:** Thomas Merton

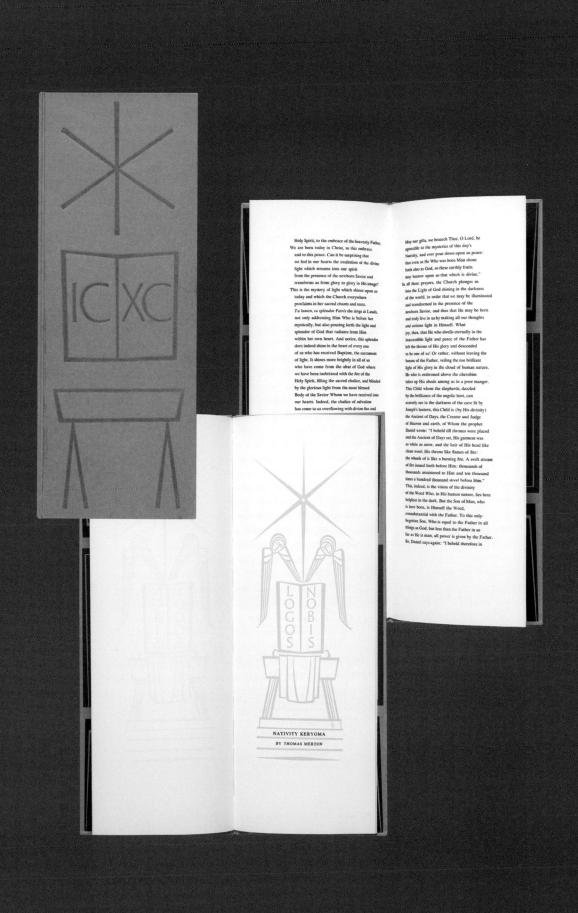

Holy Spirit, to the embrace of the heavenly Father. We are born today in Christ, to this embrace and to this peace. Can it be surprising that we feel in our hearts the exaltation of the divine light which streams into our spirit from the presence of the newborn Savior and transforms us from glory to glory in His image? This is the mystery of light which shines upon us today and which the Church everywhere proclaims in her sacred chants and texts. *Tu lumen, tu splendor Patris* she sings at Lauds, not only addressing Him Who is before her mystically, but also pouring forth the light and splendor of God that radiates from Him within her own heart. And notice, this splendor does indeed shine in the heart of every one of us who has received Baptism, the sacrament of light. It shines more brightly in all of us who have come from the altar of God where we have been inebriated with the fire of the Holy Spirit, filling the sacred chalice, and blinded by the glorious light from the most blessed Body of the Savior Whom we have received into our hearts. Indeed, the chalice of salvation has come to us overflowing with divine fire and

May our gifts, we beseech Thee, O Lord, be agreeable to the mysteries of this day's Nativity, and ever pour down upon us peace: that even as He Who was born Man shone forth also as God, so these earthly fruits may bestow upon us that which is divine." In all these prayers, the Church plunges us into the Light of God shining in the darkness of the world, in order that we may be illuminated and transformed in the presence of the newborn Savior, and thus that He may be born and truly live in us by making all our thoughts and actions light in Himself. What joy, then, that He who dwells eternally in the inaccessible light and peace of the Father has left the throne of His glory and descended to be one of us! Or rather, without leaving the bosom of the Father, veiling the too brilliant light of His glory in the cloud of human nature, He who is enthroned above the cherubim takes up His abode among us in a poor manger. This Child whom the shepherds, dazzled by the brilliance of the angelic host, can scarcely see in the darkness of the cave lit by Joseph's lantern, this Child is (by His divinity) the Ancient of Days, the Creator and Judge of Heaven and earth, of Whom the prophet Daniel wrote: "I beheld till thrones were placed and the Ancient of Days sat, His garment was as white as snow, and the hair of His head like clean wool; His throne like flames of fire: the wheels of it like a burning fire. A swift stream of fire issued forth before Him: thousands of thousands ministered to Him and ten thousand times a hundred thousand stood before Him." This, indeed, is the vision of the divinity of the Word Who, in His human nature, lies here helpless in the dark. But the Son of Man, who is here born, is Himself the Word, consubstantial with the Father. To this only-begotten Son, Who is equal to the Father in all things as God, but less than the Father in so far as He is man, all power is given by the Father. So, Daniel says again: "I beheld therefore in

NATIVITY KERYGMA

BY THOMAS MERTON

TURN

SUBVE₹TING THE ₹ELIGIOUS ₹IGHT
REPRESENTING ALTERNATIVE PERSPECTIVES OF CHRISTIANITY

JOHN RITTER
CENTERED

IN A WAY, MY FAITH WAS
ANOTHER WAY FOR ME TO REBEL.

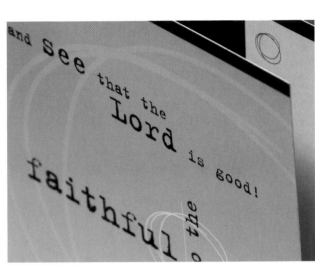

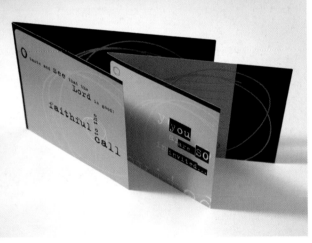

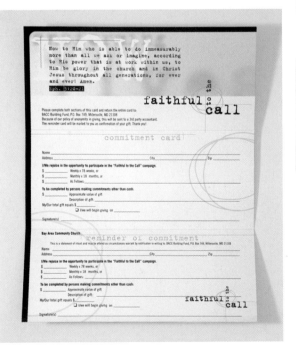

(*This Page*) **FAITHFUL TO THE CALL CAMPAIGN**[‡]
Client: Bay Area Community Church **Agency:** Exclamation
Communications, Inc. **Art Direction:** Valerie Cochran
Design: Valerie Cochran, Renee Farnie
Photography: Valerie Cochran, Colin Day

(*Opposite Page*) **TURN MAGAZINE**[‡]
Art Direction/Design/Copy: David Kasparek
Illustration: David Kasparek, John Ritter

TYPOGRAPHY, TRADITION, AND TIMELESSNESS

Typography and tradition are virtually inseparable. It would be impossible to produce a new typographic work today without relying upon conventions that have been hundreds of years in the making. Generations of artists and artisans have passed down treasures of typographical wisdom that would be hard to improve upon. They perfected the ways in which eye and hand encounter the printed word, and many of the conventions they left us are still relevant today, quite simply because they work. The typographic traditions of many of this world's surviving religious texts are precious legacies that embody practices worthy of continuation and renewal.

There exists in the design profession today an almost pathological need for individuality, for newness. The advertising culture encourages us to toss out the old to make room for the new, an endless cycle in which any regard for tradition becomes a liability. There is a misguided assumption that presumes newer is better. Yet so often this is not the case. Graphic designers are often caught up in works that have little or no lasting value. These disposable works become a canvas for the self-expression of the designer and the client, who may strive to convey personal styles that are not without their vanities.

When designing for religion, however, the graphic designer is often asked to work with content that is considered timeless. The ageless truths and enduring symbols of faith are in stark contrast with a consumer society and a marketplace that tell us to look forward and dispose of the past. The absence of valued tradition in the commercial world leaves a vacuum for many. Societies can't function without tradition, and the human soul hungers for it. This is why designers must see the typographic traditions of faith as foundations upon which meaningful design can be built. When people become more connected with where they've been, they are able to move forward with stronger intent.

"All typography implies tradition and conventions. *Tradio* derives from Latin *trado*, 'I hand over.' *Tradition* means 'handing over,' 'delivering up,' 'legacy,' 'education,' 'guidance.' *Convention* derives from *convenio*, 'to come together,' and means 'agreement.'"

—Jan Tschihold, *The Form of the Book: Essays on the Morality of Good Design*, 23.

THE SAINT JOHN'S BIBLE

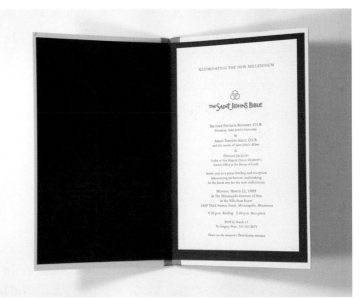

ST. JOHN'S BIBLE LOGO AND INVITATION ‡ **Client:** The Hill Museum & Manuscript Library, SJU
Agency: Design Guys   **Art Direction:** Steve Sikora   **Design:** Amy Kirkpatrick

THE STORY OF BALAAM'S ASS

I like to think sometimes of Balaam's ass.
She had more sense than her ambitious lord
who could not see the danger in the pass
when the stern angel met them with a sword.
Balaam had learning; was an eminent seer.
He looked before and after and between
with such profound discernment it was clear
that what he could not see could not be seen.
And yet, the donkey saw the angel's wrath
when Balaam only saw what he could see.
With kicks and blows he urged her to the path
and thereby shares the immortality
of that delightful beast who lives to fame
because of her sagacious tongue and eye.
Although anonymous, she shares the name
of the great prophet doomed in shame to die.
He uttered marvels, but he missed their glory.
Better to be the donkey in this story.

She took a bunch of ordinary white
and yellow zinnias, put them in a bowl,
arranged them in a ring of yellow sunlight,
but this configuration of her soul
was lost on them. Absorbed in the strict play
of wit, they did not see the bowl of flowers
that dropped under the surface lights and lay
deeply submerged during a space of hours
that had no place for flowers. Yet when the dull
thin vocables had dried among the lees
in teacups, and the indecipherable
notations on the edge of their unease
faded in ashtrays, they were surprised to find
the zinnia image floating in the mind.

STILL LIFE IN THE FACULTY ROOM

(*Top*) **OXFORD LECTERN BIBLE, 1935 Client:** Oxford,
Printed at the University Press **Design:** Bruce Rogers, typographer

(*Bottom*) **THE ANIMAL'S CAROL AND OTHER POEMS, 1976**
Client: North Central Publishing Co. **Design:** Frank Kacmarcik

Photos: © The Hill Museum & Manuscript Library, Arca Artium collection, St. John's University

✠ Communicántes, et memóriam venerántes, in primis gloriósæ semper Vírginis Maríæ, Genetrícis Dei et Dómini nostri Iesu Christi: sed et beáti Ioseph, eiúsdem Vírginis Sponsi, et beatórum Apostolórum ac Mártyrum tuórum, Petri et Pauli, Andréæ, Iacóbi, Ioánnis, Thomæ, Iacóbi, Philíppi, Bartholomǽi, Matthǽi, Simónis et Thaddǽi: Lini, Cleti, Cleméntis, Xysti, Cornélii, Cypriáni, Lauréntii, Chrysógoni, Ioánnis et Pauli, Cosmæ et Damiáni: et ómnium Sanctórum tuórum; quorum méritis precibúsque concédas, ut in ómnibus protectiónis tuæ muniámur auxílio. Iungit manus. Per eúndem Christum Dóminum nostrum. Amen.

Tenens manus expansas super oblata, dicit:

Hanc igitur oblatiónem servitútis nostræ, sed et cunctæ famíliæ tuæ, quǽsumus, Dómine, ut placátus accípias: diésque nostros in tua pace dispónas, atque ab ætérna damnatióne nos éripi, et in electórum tuórum iúbeas grege numerári. *Iungit manus.*

Quam oblatiónem tu, Deus, in ómnibus, quǽsumus, *signat ter super oblata,* bene ✠ díctam, adscríp ✠ tam, ra ✠ tam, rationábilem, acceptabilémque fácere dignéris: *signat semel super hostiam,* ut nobis Cor ✠ pus, *et semel super calicem,* et Sánguis fiat dilectíssimi Fílii tui, *iungit manus,* Dómini nostri Iesu Christi.

Qui prídie quam paterétur, *accípit hostiam,* accépit panem in sanctas ac venerábiles manus suas, *elevat óculos ad cælum, et elevátis óculis in cælum ad te Deum Patrem suum omnipoténtem, caput inclinat,* tibi grátias agens, *signat super hostiam,* bene ✠ díxit, fregit, dedítque discípulis suis, dicens: Accípite, et manducáte ex hoc omnes.

Tenens ambabus manibus hostiam inter índices et pollices, profert verba consecrationis distincte et attente super hostiam, et simul super omnes, si plures sint consecrandæ.

Hoc est enim Corpus meum.

Quibus verbis prolatis, statim hostiam consecratam genuflexus adorat: surgit, ostendit populo, reponit super corporale, et genuflexus iterum adorat: nec amplius pollices et indices disiungit, nisi quando hostia tractanda est, usque ad ablutiónem digitorum. Tunc, detecto calice, dicit:

Simili modo postquam cenátum est, *ambabus manibus accipit calicem, accípiens et hunc præclárum cálicem in sanctas ac venerábiles manus suas: item caput inclinat,* tibi grátias agens, *sinistra tenens calicem, dextera signat super eum, bene ✠ díxit, deditque discípulis suis, dicens:* Accípite, et bíbite ex eo omnes.

Profert verba consecrationis super calicem attente et continuate, tenens illum parum elevatum.

Hic est enim Calix Sánguinis mei, novi et ætérni testaménti: mystérium fídei: qui pro vobis et pro multis effundétur in remissiónem peccatórum.

Quibus verbis prolatis, deponit calicem super corpo dicens:

Hæc quotiescúmque fecéritis, in mei mem

Genuflexus adorat: surgit, ostendi et genuflexus iterum adorat:

ALLELUIA

cf. Matthew 4:23

℟. Alleluia, alleluia.
Jesus proclaimed the Gospel of the kingdom
and cured every disease among the people.
℟. Alleluia, alleluia.

GOSPEL

Matthew 15:21-28   O woman, great is your faith!

✠ A reading from the holy Gospel according to Matthew

At that time, Jesus withdrew to the region of Tyre and Sidon.
And behold, a Canaanite woman of that district came and called out,
"Have pity on me, Lord, Son of David!
My daughter is tormented by a demon."
But Jesus did not say a word in answer to her.
Jesus' disciples came and asked him,
"Send her away, for she keeps calling out after us."
He said in reply,
"I was sent only to the lost sheep of the house of Israel."
But the woman came and did Jesus homage, saying, "Lord, help me."
He said in reply,
"It is not right to take the food of the children
and throw it to the dogs."
She said, "Please, Lord, for even the dogs eat the scraps
that fall from the table of their masters."
Then Jesus said to her in reply,
"O woman, great is your faith!
Let it be done for you as you wish."
And the woman's daughter was healed from that hour.

The Gospel of the Lord.

121A TWENTY-FIRST SUNDAY IN ORDINARY TIME

FIRST READING

Isaiah 22:19-23   I will place the key of the House of David upon his shoulder.

A reading from the Book of the Prophet Isaiah

Thus says the LORD to Shebna, master of the palace:
"I will thrust you from your office
and pull you down from your station.
On that day I will summon my servant
Eliakim, son of Hilkiah;
I will clothe him with your robe,
and gird him with your sash,
and give over to him your authority.
He shall be a father to the inhabitants of Jerusalem,
and to the house of Judah.
I will place the key of the House of David on Eliakim's shoulder;
when he opens, no one shall shut
when he shuts, no one shall open.
I will fix him like a peg in a sure spot,
to be a place of honor for his family."

The word of the Lord.

RESPONSORIAL PSALM

Psalm 138:1-2, 2-3, 6, 8

℟. (8bc) Lord, your love is eternal; do not forsake the work of your hands.

I will give thanks to you, O LORD, with all my heart,
for you have heard the words of my mouth;
in the presence of the angels I will sing your praise;
I will worship at your holy temple.
℟. Lord, your love is eternal; do not forsake the work of your hands.

(Top) **ROMAN MISSAL, 1964 Client:** National Catholic Welfare Conference, Inc. **Design:** Frank Kacmarcik

(Bottom) **LECTIONARY, 1998 Client:** The Liturgical Press **Design:** Frank Kacmarcik

Although tradition may be conveyed through image or style, typography is a particularly apt medium through which traditions may be mined and explored. Typography is often the component of a design in which tradition can be most felt and experienced. It is the most accessible medium because it is meant for all who are able to read. The mere presence of a single classic typeface can offer solid ground on which a newer vision may take root. When working with religious content, it is the designer's responsibility to illuminate the sanctity of the message, to reveal its timelessness. One must take care to avoid coercing a design solution into serving the needs of one's ego or personal style. There is something not right about a timeless religious truth wrapped in a package of vanity.

Tradition is not to be confused with nostalgia, history, or a dated visual style. When embracing tradition as it pertains to graphic design, the goal is not necessarily to create a traditional look, a design hat mimics literal tradition. One must avoid attempts at fake nostalgia. The goal, rather, is to create a design informed by tradition, inspired by a time-tested perspective, a solution that can still look forward while honoring where one has been. As the guardians of tradition, designers today have the opportunity to deliver to worshippers a sense of continuity with all those who have gone before us. By connecting worshippers with where they've already been, worshippers may be better prepared to progress. Through typography, one is able to participate in a rich history deeply influenced by explorations of the divine. Letterforms whose roots can be traced back to the chiseled stone lettering of the Romans or the calligraphic handwriting of the Moors are still in wide use today.

"Experiments aimed at creating something different may be fascinating and entertaining, at least for the experimenter. But a lasting tradition will not spring from experiments. Only the legacy of true mastery can provide this."

—Jan Tschihold, *The Form of the Book: Essays on the Morality of Good Design*, 32.

FLOCK OF SHEEP ADVERTISEMENT[‡] **Client:** Trinity Presbyterian Church, Fairfield, OH
Agency: Huber+Co. **Design/Copy:** Brian Huber

SUNDAYS AND SEASONS (WORSHIP PLANNING RESOURCE), '02–'04 **Client:** Augsburg Fortress
Agency: KantorGroup **Art Direction:** Daniel Kantor **Design:** Jennifer Spong **Illustration:** Tanja Butler

Flock of
SHEEP
seeking a
SHEPHERD

Youthful congregation seeking
energetic, communicative Pastor

Full-time position offers excellent salary, housing and
car allowance, benefits and community activity fees.
Qualified candidates should submit their résumé and
sermon tape to PNC: Trinity Presbyterian Church,
6081 Ross Road, Fairfield, Ohio 45014 or email:
PNC@trinity-fairfield.com.

For complete details about the position
visit www.trinity-fairfield.com.

TEXT AS IMAGE

While the underlying elements and techniques of good typography are often those the reader will never notice, the letterforms of typography can serve as vehicles for powerful visual expression. A simple word, when given imagistic form, may become a visual celebration through which the word may be opened to new meaning. Letterforms that are traditionally reserved for practical editorial purposes may also serve as mediators that blur the line between text and image. When the visual structure of a word becomes a canvas on which other imagery takes root, both word and image become one. The viewer is able to experience meaning while also engaging a process of meaning-making.

Designers must be willing to aid the viewer in making an intuitive connection between stylized letterforms and their intended meaning or the resulting image may be experienced as arbitrary, self-indulgent, or worse, irrelevant. When type is conveyed more as image than as text, a sense of strategic context and purpose will ideally be evident to the viewer. Today's computer technology makes type experimentation almost too easy. Letterforms, when enlarged, may take on a kind of architectural presence on the page that requires of the designer a certain sensitivity to structure and form. The nuanced details of a typeface, for example, may be virtually imperceptible to the naked eye when viewed at smaller type sizes. These same details, however, when blown up to larger display sizes, may become either beautiful or awkward, depending on the awareness and sensitivity of the artist. Decorated or stylized letterforms that take on more image-like qualities must strive to balance legibility with meaningful expression.

A keen eye is required to appreciate the rich design detail that already exists in just a single letterform. Whether you're going for a modernist or conservative look, letterforms offer the designer excellent and readily available raw material for creating renewed religious expressions. Just as in other art forms, typography presents opportunities for designers to inspire in the reader an experience of beauty, deep reflection, or intellectual challenge—it takes only a skillful designer with a respect for the power of letter, word, and page. Today's designers are called to serve as the willing guardians of tradition through which viewers may experience an abundance of timeless wisdom.

VESSEL OF JUSTICE LOGOTYPE **Client:** Islamic Society of North America
Agency: Sakkal Design **Design:** Mamoun Sakkal **Translation:** "God commands justice, the doing
of good, and generosity to kith and kin. He forbids all shameful deeds, injustice, and rebellion. He
instructs you, that ye may receive wisdom." — Quran 16:90

**ABBASI PROGRAM IN ISLAMIC STUDIES
LOGOTYPE** **Client:** Stanford University, Abbasi Program
in Islamic Studies **Agency:** Sakkal Design
Design: Mamoun Sakkal **Translation:** The organization's
Arabic name is written in the Nastaliq style to reflect the
focus on Islamic studies in Iran, Pakistan, and Afghanistan
where this style of calligraphy is revered.

LUSAKA MUSLIM SOCIETY LOGOTYPE
Client: Lusaka Muslim Society **Agency:** Sakkal Design
Design: Mamoun Sakkal **Translation:** The name
of the organization is written in Arabic in a style that
appeals to Muslims in Africa.

pon them, what every man should take. And it was the
our, & they crucified him. And the superscription of
sation was written over, THE KING OF THE JEWS.
h him they crucify two thieves; the one on his right
d the other on his left. And the scripture was ful-
ich saith, And he was numbered with the trans-
And they that passed by railed on him, wagging
and saying, Ah, thou that destroyest the temple,
t it in three days, Save thyself, and come down
ss. Likewise also the chief priests mocking said
elves with the scribes, He saved others; himself
. Let Christ the King of Israel descend now
that we may see and believe. And they that
with him reviled him. ✸And when the sixth
there was darkness over the whole land until
Eloi, Eloi, lama sabachthani? which is,
My God, my God, why hast thou forsaken
hem that stood by, when they heard it,
th Elias. And one ran and filled a spunge
ut it on a reed, and gave him to drink,
s see whether Elias will come to take
cried with a loud voice, and gave up
of the temple was rent in twain from
nd when the centurion, which stood
t he so cried out, and gave up the
man was the Son of God. There
on afar off: among whom was
y the mother of James the less and
also, when he was in Galilee, fol-
unto him;) and many other
him unto Jerusalem.
24

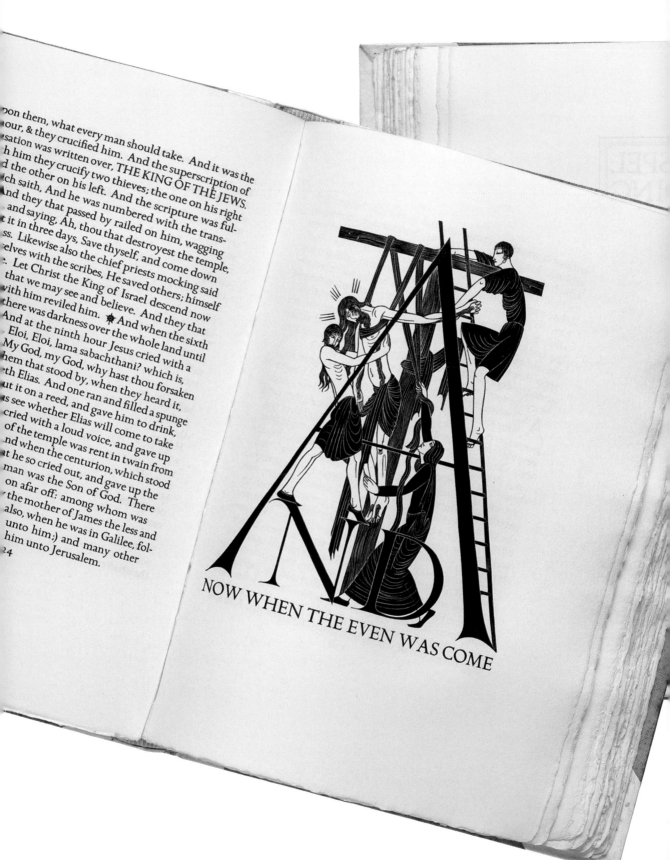

NOW WHEN THE EVEN WAS COME

160

FORASMUCH AS MANY HAVE TAKEN IN HAND TO SET FORTH IN ORDER A DECLARATION OF THOSE THINGS WHICH ARE MOST SURELY BELIEVED AMONG US, EVEN AS THEY DELIVERED them unto us, which from the beginning were eyewitnesses, and ministers of the word; It seemed good to me also, having had perfect understanding of all things from the very first, to write unto thee in order, most excellent Theophilus, That thou mightest know the certainty of those things, wherein thou hast been instructed.

THERE WAS IN THE DAYS OF HEROD, THE KING OF JUDÆA, A CERTAIN PRIEST NAMED ZACHARIAS, OF THE COURSE OF ABIA: AND HIS WIFE WAS OF THE DAUGHTERS OF Aaron, and her name was Elisabeth. And they were both righteous before God, walking in all the commandments and

131

THE FOUR GOSPELS, 1931 **Client:** Golden Cockerel Press **Design/Illustration:** Eric Gill
Photos: © The Hill Museum & Manuscript Library, Arca Artium collection, St. John's University

LOVE AND JOY BOOKLET Design: Ben Shahn

Photos: © The Hill Museum & Manuscript Library, Arca Artium collection, St. John's University

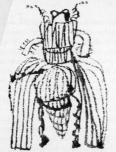

Let Anna bless God with the Cat, who is worthy to be
presented before the throne of grace, when he has
trampled upon the idol in his prank.
Let Benaiah praise with the Asp—to conquer malice is
nobler, than to slay the lion.
Let Barzillai bless with Snail—a friend in need is as the
balm of Gilead, or as the slime to the wounded bark.
Let Joab with the Horse worship the Lord God of Hosts.

Let Zadok worship with the Mole—before honour is
humility, and he that looketh low shall learn.
Let Gad with the Adder bless in the simplicity of the
preacher and the wisdom of the creature.
Let Tobias bless Charity with his Dog, who is faithful,
vigilant, and a friend in poverty.

14

JUBILATE AGNO BOOKLET, 1956 **Client:** Harvard University Press,
Fogg Art Museum **Design:** Ben Shahn **Poet:** Christopher Smart (1722–1771)

CHERRY TREE LEGEND BOOKLET, 1953 **Client:** Museum of
Modern Art, New York **Design:** Ben Shahn

THE RAGAMUFFIN GOSPEL[‡] **Client:** Multnomah Publishers
Agency: The DesignWorks Group **Art Direction:** Jason Myhre,
David Kopp **Design:** Charles Brock

**HOLY BIBLE,
BOTTS ILLUSTRATED EDITION**‡
Client: Tyndale House Publishers
Art Direction/Design/Illustration/Calligraphy:
Timothy R. Botts

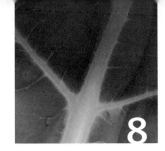

8

The Gift of Beauty

WE LIVE IN AN AGE in which beauty in all forms falls victim; it has become
a commodity to be exploited or plundered with little regard. Vast forests and prairies are
flattened and replaced by strip malls and freeways. Loud signage, cold industrial lighting,
and disposable architecture dominate sightlines once graced by gifts of nature. Many of
the world's public spaces are inundated with branded messages that offer little in the way
of visual hospitality or grace. Our homes and places of work are equally saturated by
commercial demands for our attention and allegiance.

The modern world is overwhelmed by noise, both visual and aural. We are now
exposed to so many unsolicited commercial messages and media that we spend more
time than ever before filtering what we take in. As a result, the human eye has become
much more discerning and is able to filter with startling immediacy any messages that
appear irrelevant or too demanding. "The visual, as well as the verbal, overload of
modern people requires that all the senses, and especially vision, act much more as 'data
reduction agencies' than as windows. It is likely that our capacity for vision is—or will
shortly be—congenitally fatigued by the sheer volume of images with which most
modern people cope." [14]

14. Miles, *Image as Insight*, 9.

We are so strongly affected by the barrage of societal noise that we seek shortcuts
to meaning that can simplify and distill the onslaught of information. As consumers,
we make instant subconscious purchase decisions based on the presence (or absence)
of a simple logo the size of a pea. The mere color and shape of a stop sign can lead
to an increase in blood pressure. We settle for, and sometimes prefer, approximations
of ideas rather than complete stories because we no longer have the capacity to sit still
long enough to deeply listen.

Our impatience with information is likely proportionate to its sheer volume and perhaps also to the lack of visual hospitality through which much of this information is delivered. It comes as no surprise to anyone today that many commercial messages are not entirely true or beautiful. Veiled attempts to seduce through false beauty have become so transparent, so commonplace, that even messages with the best of intentions have a difficult time getting through.

Just as children learn the grammar—good or bad—that they hear most often, visual literacy is informed by what is most often seen. Exposure to enough visual mediocrity over a long enough period of time can lead to blind acceptance, familiarity, and, finally, participation. Yet what is familiar is not necessarily healthy. The surfeit of ugliness that permeates so much of one's visual experience can have a numbing, deadening effect on the senses. It is harder to awaken to beauty when one's defenses are up, when so much energy is put toward filtering. As the noise of the commercial world strengthens its hold on us and as visual literacy wanes, these influences threaten to permeate and even to dominate our sacred experiences.

From intrusive advertisements to mailboxes filled with junk mail, graphic design at its worst is the vehicle behind much of the world's noise. This presents a moral and theological dilemma for religions employing graphic design today; the world doesn't need more noise. What the world does need is something graphic design and religions are uniquely positioned to offer: *beauty*. Graphic design is the medium through which any faith-based organization can make a noticeable, contrasting difference if efforts first originate from a more conscious, enlightened state of mind and heart. A renewed set of standards for this medium must be built upon an affirmation of beauty through which the recipient may experience enlivened truths and deep generosity. These are not qualities one often finds in commercial graphic design.

"The fact is that God is beautiful and the church is hiding this…For without a positive theological evaluation of beauty there is no motive to delight in God and no compelling reason to love Him."

—Harries, *Art and the Beauty of God*, 6.

THE POCKET CANONS Client: Grove Press **Design:** Paddy Cramsie

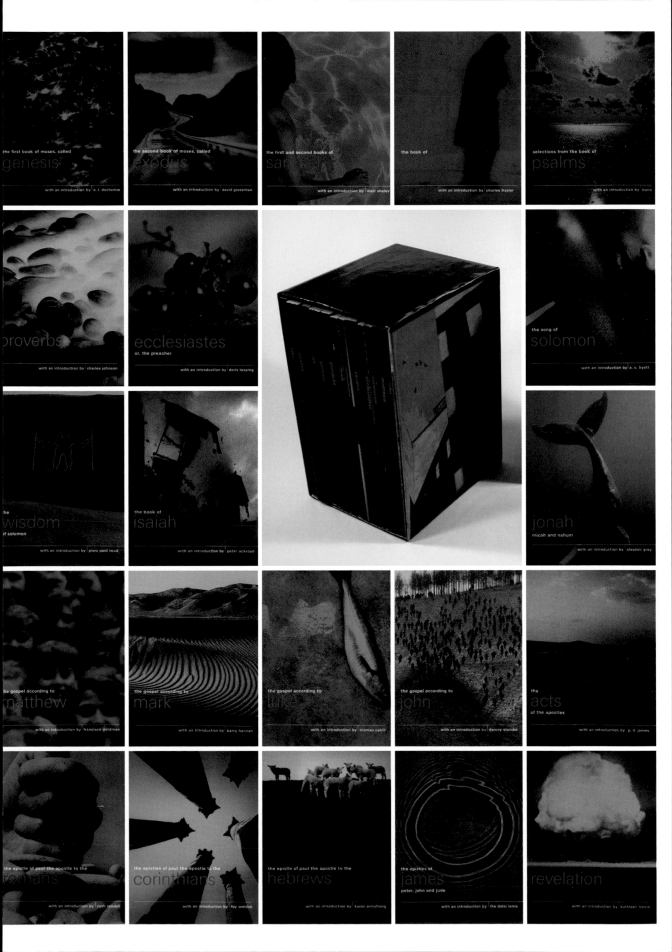

BEAUTY, THE ESSENCE OF A UNIFYING GOD

15. Harries, 42.

"If God is the giver of all good gifts and contains within himself all possible perfections, then he must be beauty as much as he is goodness and truth." [15] Graphic designers serving faith-based organizations today too often fail to acknowledge that the faith traditions they serve are built upon theological reflections of divinity suffused with transcendent beauty. It is through the visible and tangible beauty of these faith traditions that the beauty of the invisible, transcendent beyond may be approached. It is through this beauty that God's truth and goodness may be revealed and made known in this world. Beauty, then, is inseparable from the truth, love, and goodness of God, its ultimate source. It is the unity of all these things at once. One cannot approach God without the willingness to receive God's beauty. Since ancient times, the inviting grace of beauty has been an essential component and focal point of religious thought.

Commercial graphic design is driven by motives and conditions that serve the ultimate goals of the communicator rather than the viewer, and this is appropriate. The motives may be to generate a fair profit, to win allegiance, or to persuade the viewer to take a particular course of action.

Design in service of religion, however, has the opportunity to offer something altogether different, a gift of visual hospitality that allows one to encounter beauty with no conditions and to experience "joy through perception." If graphic design in service of religion is to remain concerned with matters of God or truth, it must be concerned with beauty. "If God is Beauty, then the revelation of God is a revelation of beauty and must itself be beautiful." [16] Graphic designers serving faith must first serve beauty, because to serve beauty is to reveal God. It is an offering that mirrors God's unconditional gift of beauty to this earth.

16. Richard Viladesau, *Theology and the Arts* (New York: Paulist Press, 2000), 227.

All forms of beauty are vivid examples of unity, for beauty cannot exist without it. From the created order of a symphony to the mystic wonder of a mountain range, beauty is predicated on the concord, balance, and connectedness of its component parts. The presence of unity is a sign that humility has won over ego, that harmony has won over disharmony. It demonstrates that a grouping of things or ideas, such as people, objects, design elements, or musical notes, may come together and point not to themselves but to something beyond the sum of the parts.

(Top) **SKY RAPIDS** Illustration: Gregory Houston Description: This Buddhist image expresses the inherent playfulness and self-liberated quality of energy as it is.

(Bottom) **MIND BLOSSOM SUNRISE** Illustration: Gregory Houston Description: A mandala representing the radiance of wisdom energy.

171

1

2

3

4

(All) **BOOK COVERS** Art Direction/Design: Reza Abedini

1. RESALE-YE SE ASL (THREE PRINCIPLES TREATISE) **Client:** Rozane Publications **Description:** Most of the philosophical texts in Islamic philosophy, especially in the Iranian tradition, are a deep and fine combination of religion and philosophy. Here old handwritings of last centuries' gnostics were used along with Iranian temple tile patterns.

2. FORTY NARRATIONS **Client:** Sahat Publications **Description:** Descriptions of the narrations of Islam's prophets and imams.

3. FAVAED OL-FOVAD (PROFITS OF THE HEART) **Client:** Rozane Publications **Description:** This book consists of different anecdotes on mysticism.

4. TARJOMAN-OL ESHRAGH (INTUITION'S DRAGOMAN) **Client:** Rozane Publications **Description:** A book from one of the great Iranian Gnostics, Mohi Al-Din Ebn-e Arabi, which contains very symbolic gnostic poems.

172

5

6

7

8

5. MALAMAT VA MALAMATIAN (REPROACH AND REPROACHES) Client: Rozane Publications
Description: A book about one of the Iranian-Islamic Gnostic denominations.

6. IN THE THRESHOLD OF EXALTED LORD Client: Sahat Publications Description: A gnostic translation of the words, verses, and actions of prayer.

7. DESCEND AND EXISTENCE Client: Kafa Publications Description: A religious-philosophical text about human existence and life according to religion.

8. FROM PASSION AND FLORESCENCE Client: Miras-e Maktub Publications Description: A rewrite of an old text from the 6th century about the basic principles of God's recognition.

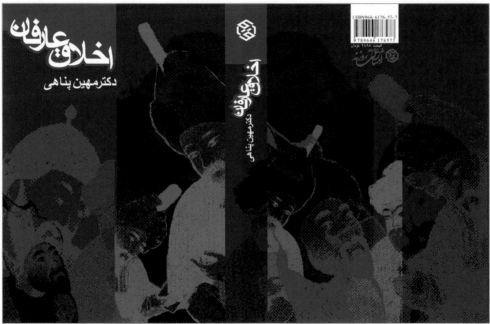

(All) **BOOK COVERS** **Art Direction/Design:** Reza Abedini

(Top) **ANIS OL-AREFIN (COMPANION OF THE GNOSTICS)** **Client:** Rozane Publications
Description: A book about the different stages and attempts of great Gnostics to gain and understand the truth of God.

(Bottom) **AKHLAGH-E AREFAN (GNOSTICS' MORALS)** **Client:** Rozane Publications
Description: A book about the relations and destinies of Gnostics as well as morals.

174

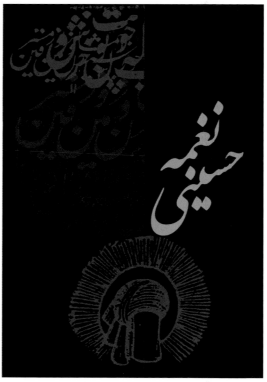

(*All*) **BOOK COVERS** Art Direction/Design: Reza Abedini

(*Top*) **BAYAN OL-ADYAN (DESCRIPTIONS OF RELIGIONS)** Client: Rozane Publications
Description: This old text introduces the different religions and Gnostic denominations.

(*Bottom*) **HUSSEINIAN SONGS** Client: Rozane Publications
Description: Poems and descriptions about Imam Hussein, the 2nd Shiite religious leader.

For graphic designers, unity is born when a conglomeration of typefaces, photographs, illustrations, papers, pixels, colors, and textures come together to form a single image. Every seasoned graphic designer has experienced the resonance of a design coming together. It is as if the individual parts vibrate in harmony and surrender their individuality. To create beauty is to gather, coalesce, and transfigure content into a whole that transcends itself. Thus, it becomes an act of transcendence, bringing the maker and viewer into connectedness with the beauty of God.

17. John O'Donohue, *Beauty, the Invisible Embrace* (Audio CD).

"When we are receptive to beauty in the world or in art, something of that harmony imparts itself to us."[17] To create beauty is not only to unify oneself with God; it is to bless those who view it. The recipient participates in the beauty of the divine fabric to which we are all connected. Creating beauty is a consecration of this world, an act of gratitude for the myriad gifts bestowed upon us that make the creation of profound beauty possible. We become beneficiaries of God's love when we encounter beauty, and we begin the journey toward a God who is not only willing to be approached but who desires and chooses to approach us. If one believes we are created in God's image, then to create is to participate in the divine creation. Beauty is the essence of who we all are. "The beautiful is really our deepest nature. We were created not to be functionaries but to be creators, and when we enter into our own creativity, then beauty becomes available to us."[18]

18. Ibid.

BEAUTY AS A CALLING

When we speak of the beautiful, our thoughts are often limited to isolated things, places, or events. Beauty is a quality we tend to notice only when it overwhelms or surprises us. John O'Donohue, Irish theologian and scholar, tells us that beauty is too often associated with "elite realms where only the extraordinary dwells."[19] Our modern perceptions of beauty only perpetuate what contemporary philosopher Peter Chojnowski considers the "house arrest" of the beautiful.[20] Beauty is too often reserved for aesthetic enjoyment alone, set apart as exclusive, or viewed through the eyes of the beholder. Thus, beauty has become a function of one's subjective feelings of contentment, prettiness, or sentimentality.

19. John O'Donohue, *Beauty, the Invisible Embrace*, printed edition (New York: Perennial/Harper Collins, 2003), 12.

20. Peter Chojnowski, "Pankalia: The Catholic Vision of Beauty," self-published article, 2002.

Beauty has not always been so subjective, compartmentalized and marginalized. From the days of the ancient Greeks through the Middle Ages, beauty had a much more encompassing presence in people's lives; it was a quality to be nurtured in one's everyday actions and attitudes. In almost all aspects of life, including education, exercise, and morality, the virtuous person was called to foster the beautiful. Beauty was as much

A LITTLE GRACE (STORYBOOK) ‡ **Client:** Grace Annabella Anderson **Agency:** Laurie DeMartino Design
Art Direction/Design: Laurie DeMartino **Photography:** Joan Buccina **Copy:** Charles S. Anderson

an activity as an outcome. It was not until the Renaissance that concepts of the beautiful began to be diminished and narrowed, designated to the domain of aesthetes and artists. The ancient Greeks did not make distinctions between artists and artisans. Concepts of beauty were intertwined with notions of thought, wisdom, intellect, and action.

In Plato's *Cratylus*, Socrates asserts that to acknowledge something through wisdom and complete understanding is to name it (*kaloun*). [21] Since the Greeks considered the works of the intellect praiseworthy and valuable, they deemed both the action of the intellect, as well as the result, beautiful (*kalon* or *kalos*). To Socrates, beauty is the product of a beautiful mind, a source of wisdom that is both human and divine. To encounter beauty is to experience this wisdom. "Wisdom is correctly given the name *kalon* (beautiful), since it performs the works that we say are beautiful and welcome as such." [22]

When we care about something we acknowledge it through its naming and thereby honor its beauty through the way in which we welcome it into our lives. We can, however, also name something through our actions. For example, we can name the profession of graphic design by simply creating beautiful works. It is through its beauty (*kalon*) that graphic design's presence is made known. It is its beauty that evokes its need to be named (*kaloun*) or *called*. Beauty, then, may be seen by artists as an invitation: we are called first to know something fully and authentically, and then we invite or *call out* and receive its beauty through our namings, actions, attitudes, and beliefs. Consider the following:

- "In Greek the word for 'the beautiful' is *to kalon*. It is related to the word *kalein*, which includes the notion of 'call.' When we experience beauty, we feel called." [23]

- The English word "vocation" comes from the Latin word *vocare*, which means "to call."

- According to Socrates, to name (*kaloun*) something was to call it forth with the fullest understanding of its inherent beauty (*kalon*). [24]

- Also from the Greeks we get *ekklesia*, which means "to call out or summon," and is rooted in the word *kalein*. From *ekklesia* we get *ecclesia*, and, ultimately, *church*. [25]

- From the Greeks we also get *kalokagothia*, which means "beauty-goodness." On this point, Plato writes: "The power of the Good has taken refuge in the nature of the Beautiful." [26]

21. *Plato in Twelve Volumes IV*, translated by H. N. Fowler (Cambridge: Harvard University Press, 1977), 416 A–D.

22. Plato, *Cratylus*, translated by C. D. C. Reeve (Indianapolis: Hacket Publishing Co., 1998), 416 D.

23. O'Donohue, 13.

24. Plato, *Cratylus*.

25. Paul Philibert and Frank Kacmarcik, *Seeing and Believing* (Collegeville, MN: The Liturgical Press, 1995), xi.

26. Plato, Philebus, 65 A.

A GIFT OF LIGHT **Illustration:** Gregory Houston **Description:** This is an expression of sacred space, of how the world might appear when perceived with pure perception.

It is remarkable that notions of wisdom, truth, goodness, call, church, and vocation may be traced back to ancient connections with beauty. These are views worthy of renewal, for we have severed our ties with definitions of the beautiful that are much more profound in their scope. Today we often confuse beauty with glamour, opulence, or decoration. We are the heirs, however, of something much more powerful and pervasive — a kind of beauty that, for more than a thousand years, humans viewed as a beacon of wisdom that could illuminate one's callings, thoughts, mind, and intellect.

Hungry hearts crave the hospitality of beauty, and people often turn to their faith traditions with the expectation of being fed. They hunger for calming insights to spiritual concerns that seem ever more relevant as the frantic pace of this planet accelerates. Consumers today spend billions in search of stress relief, spiritual awareness, and emotional harmony. In the midst of our disquiet, it is the momentary encounters with simple, authentic expressions of beauty that can offer a contrasting respite from the banal. "The vast majority of us are touched and moved by what strikes us as beautiful, especially in nature. Indeed, for many, it is the experience of the natural world that keeps them sane, which sustains and soothes them in a jarring world. The water, the grass, the calm, the sky: all help to bring peace of heart and mind." [27]

27. Harries, 3.

The call of nature is the call of God's beauty, as is the call of beautiful architecture, music, or art. The call of beauty can only be heard because we are already fluent with its language. Beauty is a deep knowing, a déjà vu of the spirit. "No one would desire to not be beautiful, because the experience of beauty is like a homecoming. When we feel and know and touch the beautiful, we feel that we are one with ourselves. Because in some subtle and secret way beauty meets the needs of the soul." [28] It is through the visual grace of creation and created beauty that the mystic world of the invisible can be engaged, and through this engagement the soul finds nourishment.

28. O'Donohue, CD.

Hungry hearts crave the hospitality of beauty, and people often turn to their faith traditions with the expectation of being fed.

It has been told that during the Soviet reign in Russia the Orthodox Church was suppressed from preaching the message of the Gospel publicly. As a way of living out their faith that "beauty will save the world" believers spent their time and precious resources to maintain and beautify their churches with detailed ornamentation and flowered landscapes. Set against rows and rows of dull, grey, and uniform government sponsored buildings, the colorfully groomed churches stood out to the people as a sign of hope and life. Many who had never heard one word about God in the public arena were moved by the beauty of the churches and brought to religious faith.

The call of beauty is both a *calling out* and a *calling forth*. To *call out* is to reveal omnipresent beauty just beneath the surface. Any artist working in service of religion can find meaning and inspiration in the belief that the beauty of the sacred is everywhere, ready to reveal itself when met by an open, willing heart. Beauty must often be coaxed out of the noise and violence of this world, but it is always there nonetheless. Graphic design is often subjected to fast-paced schedules. It is a medium easily exploited to produce mediocrity in high volume. Sophisticated systems and tools are available to graphic designers to encourage shortcuts and minimize production time. Graphic designers must remain vigilant of the effects these tensions may have on the inherent beauty of their work. They must strive to reveal the potential beauty of any project, because even with works as humble as business cards or weekly bulletins the potential to call out beauty is there.

To *call forth* is to convey to others the truth of revealed beauty. Graphic designers are not called to merely wrap content in form for their own enjoyment but to illuminate content in new light so viewers may be offered even a glimpse of something resonant with the divine. Beauty honors the God in all of us. Thus, to create beauty is an act of honesty in that it brings unified truth to light for all who encounter it.

Graphic designers are frequently involved with works that will be distributed to the public, printed in high quantities, and even distributed around the world. Graphic design is more subject to mass duplication than other art forms, and thus many eyes can quickly experience its effects in a short period of time. Its sheer ubiquity makes graphic design the medium of *calling forth*. Faith-based organizations communicate through graphic design as much, sometimes more, than many commercial organizations. If one believes in the beauty of God, the mandate for beauty in these communications is evident.

Graphic design is behind many items considered to be disposable, and, for practical or budgetary reasons, it may be argued that these items have no essential need for beauty. It's not uncommon to reserve sublime beauty for only high profile assets and initiatives like pipe organs, stained glass windows, or architecture. But one's authenticity is not expressed through the good-mannered luster of a few high profile sightlines or events. Rather, it is the cumulative effect of everyday attitudes and behaviors that forms a more honest basis for how an organization is ultimately perceived. Consider the people in your life who know you in a deep, authentic sense. Is it the people who attend only the public, peak events of your life? Or is it those who know you through your everyday words and gestures, day in, day out, year after year?

GOD IS HERE CD **Client:** GIA Publications **Agency:** KantorGroup **Art Direction:** Daniel Kantor
Design: Daniel Kantor, Kristy Logan **Photography:** Douglas Beasley

IN THE DAYS TO COME CD **Client:** GIA Publications **Agency:** KantorGroup **Art Direction:** Daniel Kantor
Design: Kristy Logan **Photography:** Daniel Furon

Churches, faith-based businesses, publishers, and religious organizations have a reason to care about the integrity and aesthetics of all of their respective communications expressions, especially those that are often considered insignificant or low priority, because these are the ultimate barometers of an organization's internal culture and values. To value the aesthetics of only the higher profile initiatives is inauthentic, even hypocritical. This suggests that a kind of opportunism may be at work seeking a return on an investment. It suggests that God, the sacred, and all things transcendent and beautiful are for special occasions and members only.

Critics of faith-based communications often experience a disconnect between the intent of the messages they receive and the poor form through which they are delivered. Graphic design, the medium so often sent forth to the broader community, can be a potent ambassador in reconciling what is professed with what the viewer actually experiences.

Many of the arts practiced within faith-based organizations are well equipped to deliver moments of intense spiritual revelation. While graphic design can do this, it is also the art form best suited to elevating content we so often fail to notice. It is a day-to-day medium able to call out much of an organization's personality. The combined effect of mailings, bulletins, advertisements, signs, and newsletters can be most revealing of an organization's true nature.

BEAUTY, AESTHETICS, AND MORALITY

Graphic design is an art form rarely seen as a tool to assist in the development of aesthetic awareness, which is necessary for any moral or religious reflection. "Morality necessarily depends in part on aesthetic discernment, on taste; taste as apperception, enabling us to recognize moral implication in aesthetic forms, as appraisal, enabling us to estimate the morally good (or bad) with the beautiful (or ugly)."[29] Aesthetic taste is required to fully participate and appreciate religion since aesthetics are so intrinsic to morality, religion, and beauty itself.

Good taste is not for the culturally elite; it is for the morally mature. To discern between something that may be morally right or wrong requires the same discernment required to interpret Scripture or a sacred icon. It requires one to become aware of nuance, the subtle as well as the concrete, context and intent. Many of life's critical questions

29. Frank Burch Brown, *Religious Aesthetics: A Theological Study of Making and Meaning* (Princeton: Princeton University, 1989), 145.

SACRED GROVE POSTER[‡] **Client:** New Era Magazine **Agency:** Church of Jesus Christ of Latter-day Saints
Art Direction: Brent Cristison **Design:** Fay Andrus **Photography:** Craig Dimond **Copy:** Shanna Butler

THE SACRED GROVE

WHAT HAPPENED HERE CHANGED THE WORLD. LET IT CHANGE YOUR LIFE.

"...we have the capacity for what is genuinely fresh, what is truly ours, for what transfigures. God is a God of beauty, and we are called to share in that beauty as we share in his work of transfiguring the world."

—Richard Harries, *Art and the Beauty of God*, 147.

involve issues that can't be viewed as black or white. It is through the arts that powers of discernment may be honed and strengthened. "The ability to reason morally grows out of a sensitivity to the immediate and particular and entails an ability to perceive the familiar in unfamiliar ways—all of which is required in the act of interpreting art and hence in the use of taste." [30]

30. Ibid.

It is precisely because so many people are now able to dabble with graphic design and because so much of our world is influenced by this art form that religions of the world have a moral responsibility to embrace a higher standard of practice and to deliver a more enlightened vision of what is possible. "It follows that failure to distinguish genuine beauty from counterfeit can lead to moral error. Moral and aesthetic discernment often go hand in hand." [31]

31. Ibid., 136.

For religion, graphic design presents frequent opportunities to offer glimpses of a deep, rich visual vernacular befitting of God's created order. We have no choice but to interact with the material world, and it is through one's experiences of this world that religious attitudes become influenced and shaped. The created world of symbols, objects, places, words, rituals, and gestures gives rise to one's aesthetic perceptions. Our interactions with religious aesthetica enable us to perceive transcendent qualities in a heightened manner. As our aesthetic discernment grows, this stimulates further aesthetic awareness, which stimulates further dialogue with the created world, and so on. The Greeks have referred to this as "the art of thinking beautifully." [32]

32. Richard Viladesau, *Theological Aesthetics* (New York: Oxford Univ. Press, 1999), 6.

"It becomes a matter of responsible action to help make available, to ourselves and others, the experience of aesthetic delight."

—Nicholas Wolterstorff, *Art in Action: Toward a Christian Aesthetic* (Grand Rapids: Ferdmans, 1980), 169.

TYNDALE BIBLES CATALOG [‡] **Client/Agency:** Tyndale House Publishers, Inc. **Art Direction:** Barry Smith

LIGHT AT GROUND ZERO BOOK [‡] **Client:** Square Halo Books, Inc. **Agency:** World's End Images **Art Direction:** Ned Bustard **Photography:** Krystyna Sanderson

EID GREETING CARDS: ARABESQUE MOON, ARABESQUE SUN **Agency:** Sakkal Design **Design:** Mamoun Sakkal

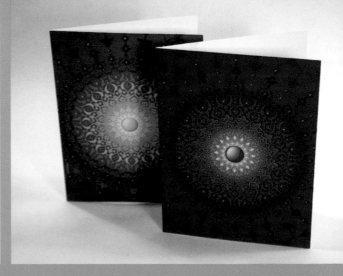

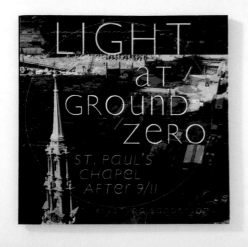

"One is not commanding all people everywhere to take pleasure in what one finds aesthetically excellent, but commending it to others on the basis of a conviction that some, and perhaps many significant groups of people with good taste, would appreciate it to a high degree, or would come to do so in time."

—Richard Harries, *Art and the Beauty of God,* 147.

SEEK MAGAZINE ‡ **Client:** Brethren in Christ Church   **Art Direction/Design:** David Kasparek   **Photography:** Andy Balc, Jay Parkinson
Illustration: Tim Hoover, Tara Dies, Mipa Lee, Mike Hioland, Jay Basinger   **Copy:** Dulcimer Brubaker

It is not uncommon for religion to make distinctions about the relative sanctity of various aesthetica used to aid in worship and communication. A business card, for example, may be seen as less sacred than a lectionary. A printed program used within a worship setting may be seen as more sacred than the weekly bulletin. These are necessary and essential distinctions to make; however, consideration must always be granted to the power of beauty. For beauty, like morality, is a virtue in itself that needs no justification. Beauty is always good for life and generative of God's presence. Often, the difference in time required to make something purely functional or to make it beautiful may only be a few minutes. In the hands of professional, it may even take less time.

If beauty is a quickener with the power to "blow the heart right open," then its opposite, the ugly, can shut one's senses down. "Ugliness dulls and deadens the spirit, marginalizes beauty as a luxury rather than a necessity." [33] Content that may be important to the viewer becomes less worthy of the viewer's attention when it is poorly packaged. This is disrespectful of the ultimate viewer and dishonors the resources of a fragile world.

If beauty, truth, and morality are virtually inseparable, then to participate in the propagation of ugliness may be seen as a moral and religious liability. Theologians have even argued that in a world with no shortage of ugliness, to create more when one has other options may be considered an act of sin or depravity. Works that may be disquieting or unsettling can still be beautiful. There is a difference between addressing dark subject matter and doing ugly work. "Beautiful works of art often include that which is disturbing and ugly, dark and disruptive. They can express violence, evoke sorrow, and depict the sordid." [34]

Like moral discernment, aesthetic determinations require a developed, mature sense of the appropriate. Within the context of graphic design, every item need not produce moments of intense spiritual revelation. Yet too often design or production shortcuts are taken, the willingness of the ultimate viewer to be challenged is sold short, and the opportunity to offer unconditional hospitality through authentic revelations of genuine beauty is lost.

33. O'Donohue, CD.

34. Harries, 22.

(Opposite Page and Following Spread) **LA PASSION DU CHRIST, 1954** **Client:** Henri Creuzevault, Paris **Design:** Bernard Buffet **Illustration:** Bernard Buffet, dry point **Photos:** © The Hill Museum & Manuscript Library, Arca Artium collection, St. John's University

Buffet was deeply marked by the Nazi Holocaust. In this book, which is a reflection on suffering, Christ is portrayed as an emaciated, shaven prisoner in a concentration camp. Note the harsh, bounded composition. INRI is tattooed on the resurrection image, which depicts Christ pinned to the shroud, still very dead. The tomb is open, however, offering the slightest bit of hope.

APRÉS LE SABBAT, COMME LE PREMIER IOVR DE LA SEMAINE COMMENÇOIT À LVIRE,
MARIE MAGDELENE & L'AVTRE MARIE VINRENT VOIR LE SEPVLCHRE. ET VOILÀ : IL SE
FIT VN GRAND TREMBLEMENT DE TERRE, CAR L'ANGE DV SEIGNEVR DESCENDIT DV
CIEL, & S'APPROCHANT RENVERSA LA PIERRE, & S'ASSIT DESSVS. SON VISAGE ESTOIT
COMME VN ÉCLAIR & SON VESTEMENT COMME LA NEIGE. LES GARDES FVRENT SAISIS
DE FRAYEVR, & DEMEVRERENT COMME MORTS. L'ANGE DIT AVX FEMMES : POVR VOVS
N'AYEZ PAS PEVR; CAR IE SÇAY QVE VOVS CHERCHEZ IESVS, QVI A ESTÉ CRVCIFIÉ. IL
N'EST PAS ICY. IL EST RESSVSCITÉ, COMME IL AVOIT DIT. VENEZ VOIR OÙ IL AVOIT ESTÉ
MIS. ALLEZ PROMTEMENT DIRE À SES DISCIPLES QV'IL EST RESSVSCITÉ.
IL SERA DEVANT VOVS EN GALILÉE: C'EST LÀ QVE VOVS LE VERREZ, IE VOVS LE PREDIS.
ELLES SORTIRENT PROMTEMENT DV TOMBEAV, AVEC CRAINTE, & AVEC GRAND IOYE,
& ELLES COVRVRENT PORTER LA NOVVELLE AVX DISCIPLES. ET VOILÀ QVE IESVS LEVR
VINT À LA RENCONTRE, & DIT : LA PAIX SOIT AVEC VOVS. ELLES S'APPROCHERENT, LVY
TOVCHERENT LES PIEDS, & L'ADORERENT. ALORS IESVS LEVR DIT : NE CRAIGNEZ POINT,
ALLEZ DIRE À MES FRERES QV'ILS AILLENT EN GALILÉE : C'EST LÀ QV'ILS ME VERRONT.

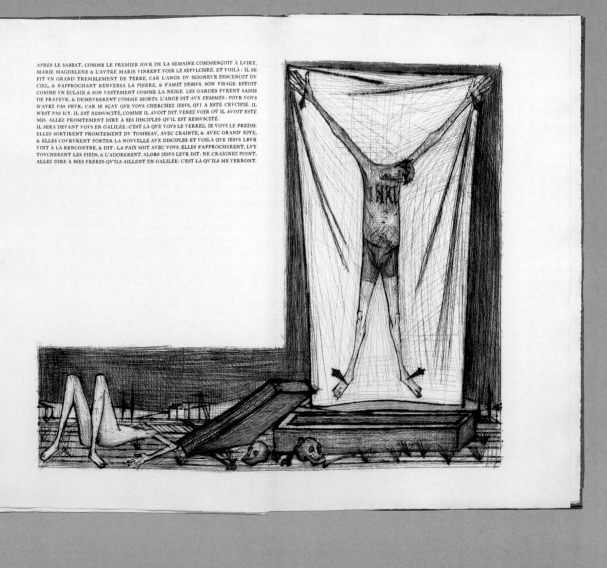

IESVS SORTIT AVEC SES DISCIPLES, & PASSA LE TORRENT DE CEDRON, AV
DELÀ DVQVEL ESTOIT VN IARDIN, OÝ IL ENTRA LVY & SES DISCIPLES.
OR IVDAS, QVI LE TRAHISSOIT, SÇAVOIT BIEN LE LIEV, CAR IESVS Y
ESTOIT VENV SOVVENT AVEC SES DISCIPLES. IVDAS ESTANT DONC SVIVY
D'VNE TROVPE DE SOLDATS & DE SERVITEVRS ENVOYEZ PAR LES PON-
TIFES & LES PHARISIENS, Y VINT AVEC DES LANTERNES, DES FLAMBEAVX,
& DES ARMES. MAIS IESVS, QVI SÇAVOIT FORT BIEN TOVT CE QVI LVY
DEVOIT ARRIVER, S'AVANÇANT LEVR DIT : QVI CHERCHEZ-VOVS?
ILS LVY RÉPONDIRENT : IESVS DE NAZARETH. IESVS LEVR DIT : C'EST
MOY. OR IVDAS, QVI LE TRAHISSOIT, ESTOIT LÀ PRESENT AVEC EVX.

QVAND IESVS LEVR EVT DIT : C'EST MOY, ILS FVRENT RENVERSEZ, & CHEVRENT
TOVS À TERRE. ALORS IESVS LEVR DEMANDA ENCORE VNE FOIS : QVI CHERCHEZ-
VOVS? ILS LVY DIRENT : IESVS DE NAZARETH. IESVS LEVR RÉPONDIT : IE VOVS AY
DÉIA DIT QVE C'EST MOY, SI C'EST DONC MOY QVE VOVS CHERCHEZ, LAISSEZ ALLER
CEVX-CY; AFIN QVE LA PAROLE QV'IL AVOIT DITE FVST ACCOMPLIE : IE N'AY PERDV
AVCVN DE CEVX QVE VOVS M'AVEZ DONNEZ. CEPENDANT SIMON PIERRE AYANT
TIRÉ VNE ÉPÉE QV'IL AVOIT, EN FRAPPA LE SERVITEVR DV GRAND PRESTRE &
LVI COVPA L'OREILLE DROITTE; ET CET HOMME AVOIT NOM MALCHVS. SVRQVOY
IESVS DIT À PIERRE : REMETS TON ÉPÉE DANS LE FOVREAV; NE FAVT-IL PAS QVE
IE BOIVE LE CALICE QVE MON PERE M'A DONNÉ?
LA TROVPE, LE TRIBVN & LES SERVITEVRS DES IVIFS PRENANT IESVS LE LIERENT.

Works that may be disquieting or unsettling...

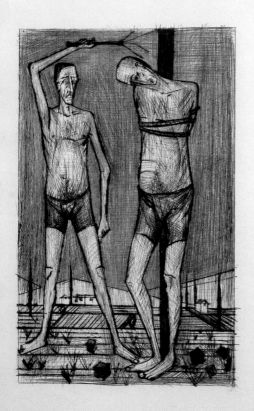

ALORS PILATE FIT PRENDRE IESVS, ET LE FIT FOÜETTER.

DEVTERONOME : « S'IL SE PRODVIT VN DIFFEREND ENTRE
DES HOMMES, & QV'ILS PORTENT L'AFFAIRE DEVANT LES
IVGES ; CELVY QV'ILS RECONNOISTRONT POVR INNOCENT
SERA IVSTIFIÉ PAR EVX ; MAIS CELVY QV'ILS AVRONT
IVGÉ IMPIE, ILS LE CONDAMNERONT D'IMPIÉTÉ. QVE S'ILS
TROVVENT QVE LE COVPABLE A MERITÉ D'ESTRE BATTV,
ILS ORDONNERONT QV'IL SOIT COVCHÉ PAR TERRE, & QV'IL
SOIT BATTV DEVANT EVX. LE NOMBRE DES COVPS SERA
REGLÉ SVR LA QVALITÉ DV PECHÉ ; ENSORTE NEANMOINS
QV'IL NE DEVRA POINT PASSER CELVY DE QVARANTE. »

...can still be beautiful.

BEAUTY AS HOSPITALITY

It is precisely the times when we least expect an offering of beauty that we are most open to being moved by it. This is when the encounter of beauty can have a startling effect on the viewer. One expects a painting or a pipe organ to be beautiful. But it is through the items we routinely experience as bland or mediocre that the opportunity for hospitality is most potent. "It is the most fleeting moments that can be the most powerful." [35] When beauty is offered not as a luxury, but as an unconditional, unexpected blessing, it becomes true hospitality, a quality rarely found in commercial communications.

Hospitality is most true when it goes beyond what is to be expected. Something as simple as an offering envelope need not be elevated to the status of a sacred icon, but it can still be iconic. It can point to something beyond itself, something that adds some much needed visual grace to the life of the viewer, and the envelope can remind us of its participation in a grander scheme. Religious organizations communicate through many messages and through multiple media forms. When working in harmony, these messages have the power to resonate with the underlying values and beliefs of the organization. Even a brochure or a Web site has the means to deliver a glimpse of the mystical, a sense of the ritual experience a particular faith community has to offer.

The cumulative effect media impressions can have on viewers is immeasurable and significant. A sign on the property of a church or temple, for example, could be viewable twenty-four hours a day, seven days a week. How many would view this sign each day? Over a decade, a medium-sized place of worship serving a few hundred people in each of its three weekly services could experience more than one million visits. Many come prepared to open themselves up, to focus their minds, and to enrich their spirits, and they are willing to receive whatever is put into their hands and in front of their eyes. These people will be handed a worship aid and a bulletin. They will be in regular contact with the Web site and on the receiving end of mailings and announcements. They'll be planning weddings and funerals using predesigned forms and guides. Other media, such as advertisements, will be representing the church in the larger community week after week after week.

When viewed as a single event, it is easy to conclude that a simple sign, bulletin, or business card isn't worth much consideration. But with a properly orchestrated communications and identity plan, a single sign or even a simple worship aid can be an integral part

35. O'Donohue, CD.

OFFERING ENVELOPES, 1959 **Client:** The Seabury Press **Design:** Frank Kacmarcik **Photos:** © The Hill Museum & Manuscript Library, Arca Artium collection, St. John's University

of a greater whole. Each item can point to the soul of the organization and signify that the beauty of God, the beauty of creation, and the beauty from which we all originate, is still alive. "One can remember that sometimes on the bleakest frontiers, where people hold out against injustice, oppression, and poverty that it's exactly that little flicker moment of beauty that enables them to endure and makes their whole struggle worthwhile." [36] Authentic beauty engages the viewer with a sense of hospitality that has no conditions. It feeds the soul with endless abundance while asking for nothing in return. Hospitality loses its light when it becomes obligatory. Religions today have the opportunity to diverge from the clamor, to become sources of visual grace that the conditional nature of the commercial world rarely offers.

BEAUTY AS TRUTH

American fast food in Hong Kong, sushi bars in Tennessee, Swedish automobiles in India, Chinese electronics in Brazil…we live in an age of homogenization, a global economy in which diverse cultures routinely exchange goods and services. Illusions are perpetuated with these cultural exchanges. One may be too willing to assume they've had an authentic cultural experience by simply dining in a Cajun restaurant or by visiting Little Italy at Disney World. Yet anyone who's actually experienced the bayous of Louisiana or taken in the vistas of Rome knows otherwise. The more global we become, the less able we are to truly appreciate and experience the cultures we so often appropriate. Instead, we've come to accept (and expect) mere approximations, samples, hints, and outlines of things infinitely more complex. As a result, cherished symbols become clichés, and rich heritage becomes fake nostalgia. The inevitable result is that our capacity to understand things more deeply is instead dumbed down; we're encouraged to believe more in shallow caricatures than in the real things.

So much of the world's noise has a false ring to it, and when something becomes less true, it becomes less beautiful. Beauty and truth are virtually inseparable, and too often religions of the world forget this. They fail to acknowledge that truths wrapped in mediocrity or ugliness become less truthful, less moral. "So beauty is in the end about honesty, about seeing what is actually there and being true to one's own response to it. Cliché, whether verbal or visual, takes what is unthought out, in short, makes it acceptable at a superficial level. But all apprehension of beauty involves a struggle to apprehend the truth, and all artistic creation involves a struggle to express it." [37]

36. Ibid.

37. Harries, 11.

KATIBE ILLUSTRATION Client: Institute for the Intellectual Development of Children and Young Adults Illustration: Reza Abedini
Description: Illustration for a magazine article about the human understanding of God.

PROPHET ILLUSTRATIONS **Illustration:** Reza Abedini
Description: Three illustrations for a text of Lebanese poet and philosopher Gibran Khalil Gibran.

Graphic design is a medium that presents many temptations to cut corners. Tight deadlines, low budgets, and inadequate training are just some of the reasons why the communications of faith-based organizations are often so disappointing. Yet the essence of religion is not concerned with the efficiency or cost-savings benefits of truth. The essence of religion must be the beauty of its truths. Graphic design is a medium often summoned to convey truth through word and image. Through beauty, the messages of religion may be delivered and received as a sign and gift of God's unconditional generosity.

BEAUTY AS RESPONSIBILITY

Environmental concerns are among the most critical issues facing the world today. No organization of good conscience, especially one involved with religion or worship, can claim to embrace the power of beauty (or social consciousness) without developing an appropriate response to the Earth's ecological crisis. From a theological perspective, humanity is not separate from God's created world but an integral part of its wonder. Such religious sensibility understands a sacred dimension to the Earth. For without the beauty of the Earth, we lose touch with a vivid presence of God's gifts, as well as the opportunity to be blessed by it and to respond to it. Through the gift of the visible world and our participation in creating it, the invisible Divine is explored and experienced.

Developers of communications media, especially printed materials, must be ever more mindful of the influences their efforts have on the environment. Graphic design is an art form that works with its own set of tools and materials, many of which can be toxic to the environment if not managed with care. The simple act of updating one's computer hardware—which is a cyclical, ongoing occurrence—requires disposal of older equipment, such as CPUs, monitors, printers, hard drives, cables, speakers, trackballs, mice, speakers, media card readers, scanners, and bulky original packaging. A typical project for any graphic designer may involve the consumption and disposal of toner cartridges, CDs, DVDs, glues, sprays, inks, laminates, and solvents.

Finally, there's paper, which is used on almost all print projects. "Paper manufacturing alone is the third largest use of fossil fuels worldwide and the single largest industrial use of water per pound of finished product."[38]* The communications activities of an organization can account for a significant percentage of annual expenditures, much of

38. American Institute of Graphic Arts (AIGA): Design Business and Ethics Series Brochure, *Print Design and Environmental Responsibility*, 5.

*For a more comprehensive discussion on the environmental impacts of graphic design, please visit: http://www.aiga.org/content.cfm/designbusinessandethics. This Web site provides a number of downloadable PDF guides. One is titled "Print Design and Environmental Responsibility." This valuable resource addresses myths and misconceptions about best practices, costs, and benefits of smart design and the use of recycled materials and soy-based inks. The guide offers dozens of links to other relevant resources on this subject.

which may go toward paper and printing. Because graphic design is a medium prone to producing so much waste, the responsibility of environmental stewardship sits squarely on the designer.

When working in partnership with religious organizations striving to remain stewards of creation's beauty, the opportunity exists to lead and innovate new design practices that are sustainable and responsible. Organizations of faith need not wait for the commercial world to lead the way.

"Now let us do something beautiful for God."
—Mother Teresa

BLISSAMBA MANDALA **Illustration:** Gregory Houston   **Description:** This stylized Buddhist lotus mandala represents purity of perception.

9

A Return to Mystery

HUMANS HAVE ALWAYS CRAVED ANSWERS. Answers are the end result of our constant quest for meaning. Answers help us feel like we have some control over the chaos of this world. Yet we all know intuitively that we can never know everything. There will always be another mystery to explore, and it is the human response to these mysteries that gives us purpose. It is through our journeys that we are often granted more meaning than is found in the end results we seek. Ultimately, it is the human capacity to explore transcendent, limitless mysteries that allows us to participate in the divine and to become more like God.

Some of the most meaningful worship experiences are able to introduce dramatic components that invite the worshipper into wondrous mysteries. This is not by chance. Indeed, the word "sacrament" (*sacramentum* in Latin) has origins in the ecclesial word "mystery" (*musterion* in Greek). Thus, the religious rituals of baptism and communion, for example, are rightly called *mysteries*. Graphic design is a medium well equipped to catalyze drama, but only if the designer is willing to keep the mysteries of the drama alive. For, without mystery, there can be no questions or healthy tension. Without mystery there can be no transcendence, no God of immeasurable love, no soul, no infinity—for these are notions one can never fully comprehend.

To strip religion of its mystery is to weaken one's need for faith. The better one is able to receive and embrace mystery in life, the stronger one's faith life can become. Religions have the means to feed the human hunger for a personal experience with the mysteries of life, death, creation, and God. By denying worshippers the mystical experiences that can heighten contemplation and reflection, religion devalues one of its most potent differentiating gifts. "Religion is an amazingly wondrous thing and is meant to be the place where the flame of wonder always lights, and where there is a space made for the mystery of the unknown. And to recognize the beautiful would return religion to its mystical depth and desire." [39]

Graphic designers usually find themselves working on projects in which they are required to remove as many questions as possible. When developing a design for a brochure, for example, the goal of the designer is not to create more mystery but to do just the opposite. Indeed, the word *graphic* means "clearly outlined or set forth." [40] To ensure a call to action, the viewer must be left with the sense that he or she knows everything there is to know about a certain product or service. In short, much secular design is concerned with doing all the thinking for the viewer. It is about *demystifying* content.

Yet when the same is done to religious works, something may be lost. For when we strip away the mysteries of religion, we lose a part of ourselves as well as God; we lose the ability to enter into invisible realms that can nourish us in ways the known, explained world cannot. This is because a mystery is different from a problem. While a problem is meant to be solved, a mystery is meant to be contemplated. While a problem is to be eliminated, a mystery is to be explored and embraced. When designing for religion, one must be less concerned with demystifying and more concerned with *remystifying*.

Mystery and truth need not be at odds, for a mystery is able to contain within it an abundance of truths that can never be fully depleted. Symbols are the means through which many of these mysteries can be approached. The ways in which symbols are interpreted and deployed by the designer can make the difference between a mystery being opened up and enlarged or its being diminished and stripped of its numinous qualities. When a mystery is made beautiful and generous, it becomes a fertile garden through which each religious believer may find his or her personal path to God and godliness. When a mystery is demystified, one is deprived of the pleasure or wisdom that can be gained by exploring its landscape on one's own.

39. John O'Donohue, *Beauty, the Invisible Embrace* (audio CD).

40. *The American Heritage Dictionary*, Second College Edition (Boston: Houghton Mifflin Company, 1982), 573.

Mystery and truth need not be at odds, for a mystery is able to contain within it an abundance of truths that can never be fully depleted.

BOOK COVER, THE OFFICE OF MATINS FOR CHRISTMAS DAY, 1955 Client: North Central Publishing Co. Design: Frank Kacmarcik

Photo: © The Hill Museum & Manuscript Library, Arca Artium collection, St. John's University

WORSHIP

FEBRUARY 1954
VOLUME XXVIII : 3

THE LUGANO CONFERENCE

WORSHIP

VOL. XXVII NO. 1 DECEMBER 1952 SEC. 1

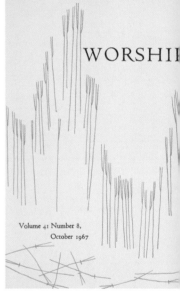

WORSHIP

Volume 41 Number 8,
October 1967

Volume 49 Number 2, February 1975

WORSHIP

WORSHIP

WORSHIP

Volume 53, Number 3
May 1979

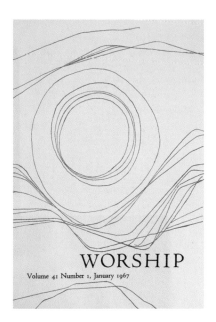

WORSHIP MAGAZINE COVERS, 1952–1981
Client: Worship Magazine, Liturgical Press
Design: Frank Kacmarcik
Photos: © The Hill Museum & Manuscript Library,
Arca Artium collection, St. John's University

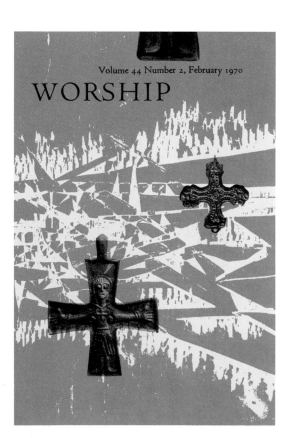

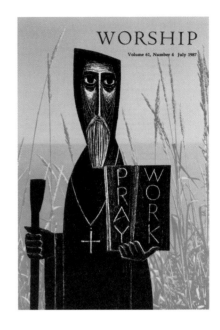

WORSHIP MAGAZINE COVERS, 1959–2002
Client: Worship Magazine, Liturgical Press
Design: Frank Kacmarcik
Photos: © The Hill Museum & Manuscript Library,
Arca Artium collection, St. John's University

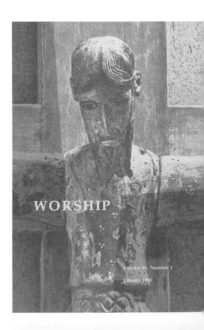

WORSHIP

JANUARY 1961 VOLUME XXXV II

worship

FEBRUARY 1961 VOLUME XXXV III

WORSHIP

May 2003 Volume 77 Number 3

Volume 46 Number 10, December 1972

WORSHIP

Volume 47 Number 6, June-July 1973

WORSHIP

Volume 45 Number 10, December 1971

WORSHIP

Graphic designers serving religion must not be afraid to introduce content that raises questions and illuminates mysteries. The mysteries of religion must not always be seen as concepts to be clarified, but as paths to personal contemplation. The designer who is willing to illuminate and enlarge these mysteries offers a gift to the viewer, for mysteries require and encourage participation. When our capacity to acknowledge mysteries is deadened, we are less able to experience the breadth of our human potential and the call to be more like God. Placing too much focus on religious knowledge and information can lead to arrogance rather than humility. As we approach the mystical, we are reminded of how vulnerable we truly are, and yet how powerful our transcendent imaginings may be. In mystery, anything is still possible, and the flame of hope is always lit.

MYSTERY AND APPROPRIATED BEAUTY

Graphic designers who are responsible for choosing the component parts of a given design are encouraged to see this as an opportunity to illuminate through mystery. When making decisions regarding photography, illustrations, typefaces, colors, and textures, the designer should consider the effect these elements will have on the symbols and mysteries being explored.

Like religion's symbols and truths, its mysteries are inherently beautiful, and thus beauty must remain an essential quality when communicating them. The temptation is too great today to use cheap stock imagery, freeware, clichés, and preprocessed content, all of which diminish mystery. There is a difference between appropriating beauty and creating it, and the conveyance of mystery demands the latter. Consider photography, for example. It seems almost anyone today can take a reasonably accurate photograph, and no one would argue that a well-taken photo of a sunset or a flower is unattractive or ugly. But is the photograph itself beautiful, or was the beauty of the subject merely appropriated? Does the photograph evoke something beyond the subject? Did the photographer interpret the subject so as to add an additional layer of created grace? Did the photographer participate in the making of the beauty?

REACH TOWARD HEAVEN CD **Client:** GIA Publications **Agency:** KantorGroup **Art Direction:** Daniel Kantor
Design: Kristy Logan **Photography:** Mark Luinenberg

There is a difference between appropriating
beauty and creating it, and the conveyance
of mystery demands the latter.

FLOWER MEDITATIONS **Photography:** Daniel Furon

"The quality of a picture is measured not by how much
it adheres to nature but by how far it departs from it."

—Paul Rand, *From Lascaux to Brooklyn*, 26.

LANDSCAPE MEDITATIONS Photography: Daniel Furon

Appropriated beauty, also referred to as *counterfeit beauty, idealized beauty,* or *beautifying naturalism* involves imagery that borrows on the beauty of the subject while offering little or no interpretive value. It places an emphasis on perfection while attempting to convince the viewer they've had an authentic experience. Counterfeit beauty is concerned with creating the illusion of the real by presenting an accurate duplicate that requires little or no thinking on the part of the viewer. Mystery is lost with counterfeit beauty because it preys on the human obsession with perfection. It leaves no room for questions and does all the thinking for the viewer.

The more sophisticated technology gets, the easier it is to produce appropriated beauty. Even cell phones have built-in cameras that, when connected with a digital printer, are able to produce images of startling accuracy. Software programs that come free on almost every computer allow users to "perfect" their images and to remove their flaws while offering no guidance as to how to reveal a subject's inner beauty. We are assaulted by predictable, overused images in almost all aspects of public life. We live in a time when shallow perfection and empty commercial images attempt to distill life's meaning down to simple, easy-to-acquire tips and techniques. "But it is just this reduction to this state of mind which an advertisement-controlled society needs. It is a symptom of the nonspiritual state of the churches that they have shown a preference for this type of beautifying naturalism."[41]

41. Paul Tillich, *On Art and Architecture* (New York: Crossroads, 1987), 30.

When one creates appropriated beauty, the human is relegated to the status of a functionary whose sole task may be to click the camera's shutter and deliver a color printout. Appropriating beauty must not be confused with *creating* beauty. Designers involved in the process of choosing art for their work are called to become more aware of the power they have to influence the quality of the raw materials. Whereas collaboration with other artists may not be an entirely new concept for graphic designers, choosing contributing artists based on their spiritual insights as well as their talent might be. Rather than choosing predictable clip art, for example, one might instead reach out to an artist who is better able to deliver an image that can go beyond itself, an image that has fresher mystical qualities. The aesthetic quality of texts may be heightened with the aid of a good writer or poet. Photography and illustration may be equally elevated by more mindful consideration.

ISA (JESUS, SON OF HUMAN) **Client:** Rozane Publications **Designer:** Reza Abedini
Description: Book design for a text of Gibran Khalil Gibran, Lebanese poet and philosopher.

**TOOBA (TREE OF PARADISE)
PUBLICATION DESIGN**
Client: Tehran Museum of Contemporary Arts
Designer: Reza Abedini   **Description:** An article
about Islamic art, the wisdom of Islamic art,
and relations between art and religion.

TA'ZIE (IRANIAN PASSION PLAY) **Client:** Rozane Publications
Designer: Reza Abedini **Description:** This book contains a selection
of photographs from one of the most important religious ceremonies
of Iranian Shiites.

Religions must work much harder today to present a contrasting vision of what is possible when it comes to communicating. Viewers have already been exposed to a broad range of very sophisticated commercial media. It is time for religions to open the eyes of a world that believes it has seen everything. In a culture that is obsessed with the false notion that humans can know and control everything, it is profoundly truthful to embrace the realities of our most powerful mysteries. It is through its mysteries that religious media can offer viewers the opportunity to participate in their own transfiguring. In a world obsessed with answers and solutions, we've forgotten that one cannot grasp any notion of the divine or the infinite without entering into the beauty and grandeur of their mysteries.

"Images of mystery build a bridge between what we see and what we believe. Through images of mystery we enter into the Divine, God's personal life where time and space are changed."

—Nicholas Markell, Iconographer and Ecclesial Liturgical Artist

MARKELL STUDIOS WEB SITE *(www.markellstudios.com)* **Client:** Markell Studios **Agency:** KantorGroup
Art Direction: Daniel Kantor **Design:** Kristy Logan **Illustration:** Nicholas Markell **Copy:** Nicholas Markell

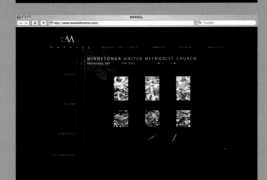

Renewing Symbols

THE HUMAN CAPACITY TO IMAGINE, communicate, create, and educate is predicated upon the ability to symbolize. For the human experience to be anything but mundane, the use and experience of symbols are required because they connect us to our greatest ideas, things, places, beliefs, and actions.

Cultures and societies cannot meaningfully function without symbols. Written languages rely on the grouping of linguistic letter symbols (words). The mind's symbolizing faculties organize emotional and mental activities and are essential components in making sense of raw information and data that, when brought together, result in ideas, concepts, perception, knowledge, and wisdom. It has even been suggested that the power of understanding symbols is "the most characteristic mental trait of mankind," [42] a power that allows us to not only imagine God, but also to become more godlike in our thoughts and actions. "The driving force of the escalator that promotes us from sensation to reflection and from reflection to constructive interpretation is the human power (that humanly mirrors the divine) to create true symbols." [43] Poetry, literature, drama, paintings, mythology, and religion cannot be fully experienced without an understanding of and appreciation for symbols.

The enlivened functioning of any religious or spiritual endeavor is dependent upon the bridge-building power of symbols. The symbol has the power to effect a connection between any aspect of the tangible, concrete present and the ineffable, the transcendent, and the infinite. Indeed, theologically something that is *symbolic* "brings together," while something that is *diabolic* "tears apart"—that which is diabolical is that which destroys

42. Suzanne Katherina Knauth Langer, *Philosophy in a New Key* (Cambridge, Harvard Univ. Press, 1957), 156.

43. Paul Avis, *God and the Creative Imagination* (London: Routledge, 1999), 104.

unity and oneness. Without symbols, it would be impossible to comprehend God or to reconcile the human irony of being constrained by the laws of physical reality, imprisoned in a way by human limits, yet still able to imagine vivid, boundless possibilities. Through symbols, the finite meets the infinite, weakness meets power, despair meets hope, and emptiness meets sustenance. Most important, symbols bring into vision that which was previously not seen or known. "Symbols are the way in which we can enter the meaning of the religious, and without them we can only distort religion."[44]

44. Tillich, *On Art and Architecture*, 36.

It would be difficult to name a profession more concerned with symbols than that of graphic design, especially when involving works that incorporate a faith or religious component. To fully serve any client, religious or secular, it is the responsibility of the designer and project participants to acquire both a humble appreciation for the power of symbols as well as an adequate understanding of the specific symbols relevant to a particular project. Neglecting to do so can lead to disastrous results. For when a symbol is abused, all that it represents, as well as those who cherish it, are also abused.

Faith traditions of every kind consider many of their symbols sacred because the symbols are seen in direct connection with the sanctity of what is represented. So when one bows to an altar, drinks consecrated wine, prays to the east, or raises one's hands up to God, it is the symbol's truth-source that is called forth and awakened. The reverence of sacred symbols is a sign of deep love and belief in the realm made manifest.

Of course, the more a symbol is loved or revered and the more power a symbol takes on, the more likely it is to be mistreated. Religious symbols are often used for mere convenience, to represent or to oversimplify rather than to open up and extend one's vision. When this occurs, the beauty and grandeur of the truths that birthed the symbol become diminished as well. This is how symbols become clichés, how images become kitsch, and how communal expression is reduced to nothing more than selfish outcry. Living symbols become deadened when those who use them fail to acknowledge and reflect upon the depths from which these symbols are birthed. When a dynamic symbol is reduced to a static sign, it becomes stringent and bound.

When one bows to an altar, drinks consecrated wine, prays to the east, or raises one's hands up to God, it is the symbol's truth-source that is called forth and awakened.

Graphic designers, especially those serving religion, must acquire a sensitive appreciation for the difference between signs and symbols. Signs are primarily applicable to static,
straightforward content. They are used not to deepen but to direct. A sign is not meant to
be ambiguous or subjective. It is not meant for reflection—a sign's purpose is to point to
something that presents few difficulties in comprehension to all who view it, things that
are already known. Signs require little or no imagination when viewed, and they can be
invented and destroyed at will with little effort.

A symbol, on the other hand, does not refer to a known, present reality but points
instead to something beyond and previously unknown that requires imaginative involve-
ment. A symbol cannot be invented or made. It must be born of that which it represents,
and it can only die when the source or essence of its truth dies. Its life is made possible
through the direct, umbilical-like connection to the vitality and substance of what it
symbolizes. A living symbol calls upon the essence of that which it points to and brings
to immanence a realm of existence that could not have been grasped or experienced any
other way. In a sense, the symbol becomes the tangible material of this world through
which the living material of another world may take form. But like any powerful tool,
a symbol is dependent upon how it is used. The way in which a particular symbol is
employed and the context in which it is used can have a dramatic effect on its ability
or inability to bring into being the realm of truth it represents.

A sign points you *to something,* while a symbol takes you *through something.* Whether
a symbol is an object, a gesture, a simple flag, or even a three-act play, it has the power to
move the participant from one state of mind to another. Within the context of graphic
design, one must be willing to see symbols of religion not just as visual opportunities to
enhance a composition or as identifying badges, but as portals through which the viewer
can take a sacred journey. The visual composition of one's design vision must be able to
accommodate not just the symbol being placed but also the grace and power of the truth
that may come forth through it. Just as a seed that is simply placed on a stone will never
grow, a symbol placed with little care or reverence can never fully bloom. To the graphic
designer the visual hospitality of a given design may be seen as a midwife who assists the
symbol in bringing its *veritas* to life. Both designer and design become participants in this
birth, as does the viewer. Seen in this light, it is no wonder that the birthing experience
facilitated by a symbol has been referred to as a "signature of God's immanence." [45]

"A sign is a thing,
object, person, or
circumstance that
represents or points
toward another thing,
object, person, or
circumstance. In
contrast, a symbol is
an action that reveals
a relationship; it is
not a thing."

—Mark G. Boyer, *The
Liturgical Environment*
(Collegeville: The Liturgical
Press, 2004), 45.

45. F. W. Dillistone, *The
Power of Symbols in Reli-
gion and Culture* (New York:
Crossroads, 1986), 11.

HARVEST FELLOWSHIP IDENTITY SYSTEM ‡ **Client:** Harvest Fellowship of Churches, Lancaster, PA
Agency: Brand Equity **Art Direction/Design:** Steven Smith

BAY AREA COMMUNITY CHURCH LOGO AND NOTE CARD ‡ **Client:** Bay Area Community Church
Agency: Exclamation Communications, Inc. **Art Direction/Design:** Valerie Cochran

FIRST UNITED METHODIST
of LaGRANGE

1828

First Assembly of GOD
OKMULGEE · OKLAHOMA

Graceworks
Lutheran Services

Graceworks
Housing Services

BethanyVillage
Graceworks Lutheran Services

Graceworks
Enhanced Living

Consumer Credit
Counseling Service
Graceworks Lutheran Services

FIRST UNITED METHODIST OF LAGRANGE LOGO[‡]
Client: First United Methodist of LaGrange **Agency:** Brant Kelsey Design
Art Direction: Brant Kelsey **Design:** Niki Studdard

FIRST ASSEMBLY OF GOD LOGO[‡]
Client: First Assembly of God, Okmulgee **Agency:** Matcha Design
Art Direction/Design: Chris Lo

GRACEWORKS LUTHERAN SERVICES IDENTITY[‡]
Client: Graceworks Lutheran Social Services **Agency:** Brand Equity
Art Direction/Design: Steven B. Smith

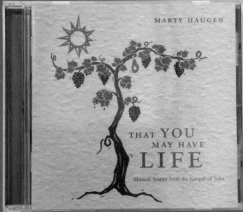

ALIVE IN CHRIST JESUS CD **Client:** GIA Publications
Agency: KantorGroup   **Art Direction/Design:** Daniel Kantor
Photography: Mike Woodside

THAT YOU MAY HAVE LIFE CD **Client:** GIA Publications
Agency: KantorGroup   **Design/Illustration:** Kristy Logan

BLESSINGS BOOKLET ‡ **Client:** WayMakers
Agency: Above: The Studio   **Design/Illustration:** Kimberly Garza

Although religion's visual symbols are conveyed through many other art forms, graphic design is the medium through which these symbols are prone to the most casual use or overuse. It is through graphic design that the visual symbols of religion are often merged with text and image. It is the medium through which these symbols are distributed to the public in the form of books, posters, and direct mailings. Thus, it is the responsibility of graphic designers to employ these symbols with reverence and care.

SYMBOLS AND MULTICULTURALISM

How does a mostly English-speaking faith community respond to a growing Asian community within its membership? How might a Somali family be made to feel welcome by a Midwestern Protestant church? Can Kwanzaa and Christmas be celebrated concurrently within the same parish?

Cultural sensitivity is required of anyone hoping to reach out to diverse ethnic or religious communities. There is no better way to welcome and embrace another community than to show respect for their cultural or religious symbols. Such efforts, however, require due diligence on the part of any designer who chooses to work with unfamiliar symbols. The desire to communicate hospitality with the best of intentions can have just the opposite effect if done carelessly. The comprehensive research of religious symbols is perhaps some of the most important work a graphic designer serving religion can ever do.

It is not uncommon for faith communities to become so immersed in their own symbols that they are unable to see objectively. Communities may become so culturally conditioned by their own symbolic realities that they are perceived as closed minded and unwelcoming to outsiders who have something new or different to contribute. Working with an outside graphic designer who sees through fresh eyes can provide necessary objectivity, and it is essential that faith-based organizations communicate to the design community that this objectivity is valued and welcome.

TURN MY HEART BOOK **Client:** GIA Publications **Agency:** KantorGroup **Art Direction:** Daniel Kantor
Design: Kristy Logan **Photography:** Douglas Beasley **Copy:** Susan Briehl and Marty Haugen

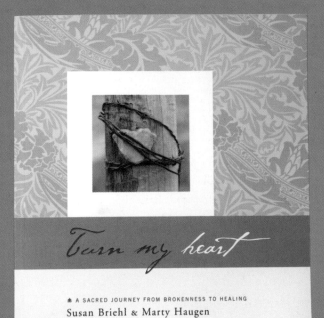

Turn my heart

♣ A SACRED JOURNEY FROM BROKENNESS TO HEALING

Susan Briehl & Marty Haugen

Healing, hoping

O God, you cradle the mountains
and hold the mighty waters
in the hollow of your hand.
You carry the weak in your bosom
and tend each leaf and living thing.

I place myself into your keeping,
my body, my soul, and all that I am,
for you are my help, you are my hope,
you are my highest praise.

Write my name upon your palm,
hold me near your side,
for by your wounds, I am healed,
and in your hands, I am home,
where all will be well.

All will be well in you.
Amen

1

2

3

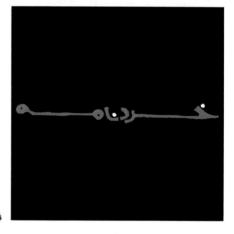

4

5

(All) **LOGO DESIGNS** **Art Direction/Design:** Reza Abedini

1. THOUGHT AND ART **Client:** Tehran Museum of Contemporary Arts

2. BAYENE (MANIFESTER) **Client:** Cultural and Quranic Association **Description:** Inspired by ancient Iranian seals.

3. SEYED HEYDAR AMOLI FOUNDATION

4. KHERAD-NAME (LETTER OF WISDOM)
Description: Logo for a philosophical-religious magazine.

5. KATIBE (INSCRIPTION) **Client:** Institute for the Intellectual Development of Children and Young Adults

6

7

8

6. ISLAMIC WORLD CALLIGRAPHY FESTIVAL
Client: Iranian Academy of Art

7. SCHOOL OF ATTESTER **Description:** Logotype for a religious society.

8. MAHBUB-MANESH **Client:** Mahbub-Manesh Foundation **Description:** Logotype for a cultural-Gnosticism foundation.

9. SEYED AHMAD FARDID **Client:** Fardid Foundation **Description:** Logo for a wisdom and philosophy foundation named after of one of the great Iranian contemporary philosophers.

10. TOOBA (TREE OF PARADISE)
Description: Logo for a cultural religious association.

9

10

SYMBOLS AND IMAGINATION

Much public discourse, especially when it pertains to religion, attempts to clarify or make literal the wonders of God and the divine. From politicians to clergy, the most pressing of human concerns are too often and too easily reduced to simple answers, factual thinking, honest truths, and precise language. Rich, abundant landscapes, which can only be fully explored by the imagination, are reduced to small tracts in which all life and mystery are stripped, where we are fed by a fast-food mentality that promises simple answers with little effort. And, when the truths of religion are diluted, so too are its symbols.

Today's graphic designers must strive to avoid the dulling of religious sacred symbols. Much of the media produced for religions involves symbols, so designers have a responsibility to act as stewards of these symbols, nourishing them and giving them new life. Symbols are not to be seen as opportunities for casual or convenient use. When the power of a symbol is appropriated for false use, the symbol becomes less truthful, and the viewer's capacity to imagine a more godlike state of enlightenment through the fullest truth of the symbol is compromised. And if one accepts that beauty and truth are inseparable, the false use of a symbol not only makes it less truthful, but less beautiful.

Symbols, when properly employed, enlighten, illuminate, and open up meaning. Like the Christian parable of the loaves and fishes, a symbol and its beauty are able to offer endless nourishment to those who encounter it while asking for nothing in return. In its purest sense, a symbol offers unconditional hospitality. False symbols instead darken and limit one's view. They are static and rigid, suggesting to the viewer one way of seeing something. One need only recall the Nazi swastika for an example of this. False symbols disengage the imagination while imposing strict interpretive boundaries, thereby requiring little or no participation on the part of the viewer. They ask for blind loyalty.

When a symbol loses its depth and wisdom, when imagination ceases to be engaged, it has become *desymbolized*. "Imagination is the milieu of symbolism…To receive what a symbol has to give us, we need to participate in it by imaginative indwelling, and that is how we are enabled to participate in the reality of what it symbolizes." [46] Many of today's religious symbols are in danger of becoming desymbolized, and graphic designers today can play an important role in their resymbolization; however, it will require a much more mindful application of these symbols and their usage. It will demand a renewed embrace of the power of the imagination.

46. Avis, 103.

(Opposite Page, Top) **CLERGY WELLNESS AND THE STEWARDSHIP OF ABUNDANCE REPORT**[‡]
Client: The Church Pension Fund (Episcopal Church) **Agency:** Jacqueline Kohn & Laura Gernon **Art Direction:** Laura Gernon, Jacqueline Kohn **Design:** Laura Gernon **Illustration (Fabric appliqué):** Lee Porzio **Copy:** Alan Blanchard

(Opposite Page, Bottom Left) **KHERAD-NAME (LETTER OF WISDOM) MAGAZINE COVER**
Client: Hamshahri Publications **Design:** Reza Abedini **Description:** A philosophical-religious magazine.

(Opposite Page, Bottom Right) **KATIBE (INSCRIPTION) MAGAZINE** **Client:** Institute for the Intellectual Development of Children and Young Adults **Design:** Reza Abedini **Description:** A magazine about religious literature.

THE GIFT
of
ABUNDANCE

CLERGY
WELLNESS
and the
STEWARDSHIP
of ABUNDANCE

ALAN F. BLANCHARD
PRESIDENT EMERITUS,
THE CHURCH PENSION FUND OF
THE EPISCOPAL CHURCH

W ELLNESS…ABUNDANCE…STEWARDSHIP…
THESE WORDS ARE IMPORTANT TO EVERY MINIST

- The mission of the Church Pension Fund importantly includes fostering w
- Our Lord has promised us abundance in the things that count.
- We are stewards of a faith, a history, and a vast array of tangible and in

The Church Pension Fund began with abundance when its founders rai
well beyond their original goal of $5 million. In 1994, the fund's trustees
opportunity to consider uses for assets beyond these required to meet their
began a 10-year process of church-wide consultation regarding the needs a
members and beneficiaries. This work led to an unparalleled array of
benefit enhancements.

The following section presents a review of the sources of this abundan
of its main uses, and a summary of the process that identified new be
enhancements. And the story is not over. As of March 31, 2005, the Chu
Assets Available for Benefits stand at an all-time high of $72 billion. So this
bration of abundance, but has two purposes beyond that. It tells a story in which the Episcopal
Church can take great pride. Equally important, it asks, what lies ahead?

"We need to recapture the sense that the ancient world had that symbols participate in and make present the reality that they signify."

— F. W. Dillistone, *The Power of Symbols in Religion and Culture*, 108.

(*Upper Left*) **SUNDAYS AND SEASONS (WORSHIP PLANNING RESOURCE), '99–'01** **Client:** Augsburg Fortress **Agency:** KantorGroup **Art Direction:** Daniel Kantor **Design:** Jennifer Spong **Illustration:** Nicholas Markell

(*Above*) **SUNDAYS AND SEASONS, '02–'04** **Client:** Augsburg Fortress **Agency:** KantorGroup **Art Direction:** Daniel Kantor **Design:** Jennifer Spong **Illustration:** Tanja Butler

(*Left*) **SUNDAYS AND SEASONS, '05–'07** **Client:** Augsburg Fortress **Agency:** KantorGroup **Art Direction:** Daniel Kantor **Design:** Kristy Logan **Illustration:** Lucinda Naylor

So much of today's world is explained to us by science, philosophy, and religion. But the true strength of religion lies not in the realm of science, but in the realm of truths dependent upon imagination. Graphic designers must always remember this, because design that engages the imagination can take the viewer on a healing journey through his or her questions about God. "The greatest truths can only be expressed in imaginative form—through images (metaphor, symbol, and myth). We know the truth only through the imagination." [47]

47. Ibid., 8

To resymbolize today's religious symbols, there is a need for a kind of spiritual radicalism through which symbols can be reborn. We must learn again to approach our most sacred symbols through the bridge-building power of the imagination, for only then are we able to connect the present with the transcendent, the possible with the imagined. We live in a time when the concept of image is emphasized by capitalism and free markets, where symbols and metaphors are casually created and destroyed while requiring nothing of the viewer but blind loyalty. "One of the greatest paradoxes of contemporary culture is that at a time when the image reigns supreme the very notion of a creative human imagination seems under mounting threat." [48]

48. Richard Kearney, *The Wake of Imagination* (London: Hutchinson, 1988), 3.

Both the secular and the religious worlds often choose to devalue and exploit the power of symbols. Many of the world's most sacred religious symbols have become like inarguable prose, rigid and divisive. They reveal not the unconditional, endless hospitality of the mystical but instead conditional, limited literalism. To resuscitate these symbols, they must be broken open. They must be probed at a deeper level to once again encounter the truth they were originally meant to reveal. A retransformation of the literal to the mystical must begin. By breaking open a symbol, it is able to become bigger than itself and challenge both designer and viewer to see in the symbol something new, something living and vital.

To break open something is to reveal its essence. Holy books are filled with opening and breaking themes. By breaking open scripture, it is kept vital. By breaking a body, it becomes a sacrament, a sacrifice. Taking something and pulling it apart allows one to get inside of it so as to be more fully nourished by it. None of these activities is possible, however, without a renewal of the imagination's role in keeping symbols vital and healthy.

WELLSPRING INTERNATIONAL LOGO AND BROCHURE[‡] **Client:** RZIM/Wellspring International **Agency:** 3HD **Art Direction/Design/Illustration:** Matt Cooley

wellspring international

Wellspring International is the eyes and ears for those whom God has burdened for the abused and disadvantaged. Our mission is to come alongside existing organizations who are aiding individuals, primarily women and children, in underprivileged situations overseas. An outreach of RZIM, Wellspring International is a tangible extension of the central focus of RZIM – a demonstration of the apologetic we teach and defend. Our goal is not just to rescue and provide a solution for a better life physically, but to point them to Christ to fulfill their greatest need.

RESCUE ... **REHABILITATION** ... **RESTORATION** ... RE-

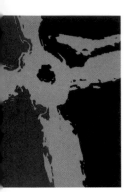

- **Minimize casual use:** Avoid any treatment of a symbol that may diminish the nature of its depth. The best use of a symbol is one in which its multilayered meaning is revealed and enhanced.

- **Beware of guidelines becoming rules:** Rules by definition are limiters. They set boundaries. For symbols to be opened up, boundaries must be challenged. Consider, for example, the Christian faith's use of red and green during the Christmas-season. These need not be the only colors used during such a rich, spiritual time of year. Blue may be paired with red as sign of Advent transitioning to Christmas. Orange paired with yellow may be a fresh way to convey the warmth and light of the Christmas star. Visual potency is often more meaningful to the viewer than predictability. Designers are the best stewards of symbols when they are able to balance their clients' needs to remain rooted in tradition while still moving forward.

- **Juxtapose:** If a symbol is the coming together of the here and now with the transcendent beyond, what elements of the beyond may be merged with elements of the present? Make a list of the elements that a symbol points to, and awaken the viewer's eye and imagination by pairing these elements together in an unexpected way.

- **Think in metaphors:** Through visual metaphors, we are able to envision one element in terms of another—family as vine, Earth as mother, shield as shelter, water as life. Metaphors are closely related to symbols and grant the viewer access to fresh, surprising experiences.

Visual potency is often more meaningful to the viewer than predictability.

- **Meet with a theologian, philosopher, art historian, or religious scholar:** Tapping the wisdom of someone with a strong academic background in divinity, philosophy, or art can reinvigorate one's assumptions and perspective.

- **Draw from personal experience:** What might a particular symbol mean to you? What personal stories might shed new light on the symbol? Has the symbol grown in depth and breadth for you, or has it lost meaning? How? Name the symbols in your life that are alive and filled with abundant meaning.

- **Research the origins of the symbol:** A symbol is a microcosm that contains entire stories. Examining the history behind a symbol will almost always lead to surprises that can inform and influence one's design. Understanding the origins of a symbol can free one from becoming stifled by the inertia of tradition.

- **Quiet your mind, meditate, reflect, pray:** To make art is to offer one's life as a channel for the beauty and energy of the divine within our midst. Yet graphic design is often a stressful activity rife with distractions. Setting aside preoccupations and establishing healthy boundaries for life's tedium can better prepare one for the kind of mindfulness required to do good work.

"Every act of creation is first an act of destruction"

— Pablo Picasso

"The words *symbol* and *church* share a common source in the Greek language and a common tendency to unify and empower. *Church* comes from the Greek word *ekklesia*, rooted in the verb *kalein*—to call or summon...The word *symbol* also comes from the Greek. *Sym-ballien* means roughly throwing together or integrating elements that had been broken apart."

—Paul Philibert and Frank Kacmarcik, *Seeing and Believing*, xi.

SEEING AND BELIEVING BOOK **Client:** Liturgical Press
Design/Illustration: Frank Kacmarcik **Copy:** Paul Philibert **Photos:** © The Hill Museum & Manuscript Library, Arca Artium collection, St. John's University

11

Building Bridges

FOR GRAPHIC DESIGN to serve religion most meaningfully, dialogue between the two disciplines must continue. Regardless of how deep one's understanding of religion or graphic design, one must remain open to the insights of both fields. Both religion and graphic design are suffused with vernacular jargon that may not be understood by novices. Grasping the language of each is a prerequisite to leveraging their strengths.

THE NEED FOR THEOLOGICAL REFLECTION

How might a book of prayer for a Calvinist congregation differ from a lectionary for a Catholic community? Is there a difference between designing a poster and designing a prayer book as a ritual object? How is the symbol of bread experienced in the Methodist tradition? The Baptist tradition? The Episcopal tradition? How might the theology of St. Thomas Aquinas be translated to an identity system for a church of the same name? What are Islamic beliefs about imagery, symbol, and worship? What does the color purple signify in a Catholic liturgy? What is the role of quietude in Buddhism?

As religions strive to offer something in direct contrast with secular consumerism, graphic designers are called to more fully appreciate the true nature of this offering. The integrity of graphic design practiced by faith-based organizations is perhaps most vulnerable when the designer lacks theological perspective. Since there are so few graphic designers who specialize in liturgy, worship, or religion, much of the work is being done by designers who lack the interdisciplinary education or the experience required to maintain appropriate tension between aesthetic and theological concerns. Whether the work is done

245

by those who lack sufficient artistic training or by graphic designers who lack theological training, the result is often less than what it could be. This is one of the reasons religious communication is so flooded with overused clip art, clichés, and catchphrases that do nothing but further distance the viewer from a deeper enrichment of his or her sense of the sacred. Without an understanding of relevant theology, designers are left to fill the void with only what is familiar, convenient, or innocuous.

Theological reflection on graphic design is required to most fruitfully bring the artist, viewer, and intent into enlivened harmony. Without an informed theological alignment of all the design elements, there can be no resulting unitive image that will open up the content with fresh relevance and potency. There can be no strategy that harmonizes multiple communications through one voice. Whether a designer is engaged to produce a new logo, a seasonal banner, or a worship aid, he or she must be provided with the necessary theological context or be given the freedom to meet with a theologian trained in such matters.

Though it may not always be possible, it is also strongly suggested that designers working on faith-based projects practice a sense of the faith, a shared reverence for the rituals and traditions being served. Effective design, particularly within worship, strives for an authentic translation of the spiritual, the numinous, the redemptive. This requires a heart of generosity, a designer willing to explore and examine his or her faith to aid the viewers in gaining a deeper sense of their own. If the designer shares no sense of value or belief in that which is so central to the intended audience, how can the contribution be received in trust? A designer must be willing to be humbled, even enchanted, by the idea that he or she is building a bridge between viewer and Maker. To do so requires exploring one's own spirituality as well, for without personal reflection the gift of your creation cannot fully shine. "It is futile to expect adequate representations of divinity from designers whose misfortune it is never to have entertained adequate notions of divinity." [49]

49. Graham Carey, "Figures of the Sacred Heart," *Catholic Art Quarterly* 15 (1951), 5.

"Open your heart, and that which is there in the depth of reality will enter your heart, and you will be able to create."

—Paul Tillich, *On Art and Architecture*, 41.

RÉQUIEM ‡ *(a senior thesis)* **Art Direction/Design/Illustration/Photography:** Lynn Fylak

DIVINE IDENTITY BOOKS
Art Direction/Design/Photography/Copy:
Erik Adams

Nearly 55,000 young men and women currently
serve as missionaries for The Church of Jesus
Christ of Latter-day Saints. While each has a
unique experience, a common journey takes
place within. The personal experiences and
thoughts of nearly 100 former missionaries,
collected through interviews from around the
world, are woven together into a composite
narrative within the pages of *Divine Identity*.
The writings of Joseph Campbell act as a
framework around which the story is told,
echoing the classic hero myths passed down
by countless cultures throughout time.

248

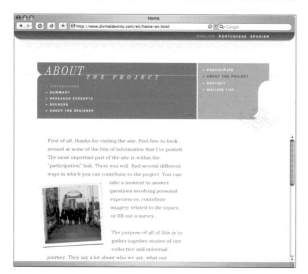

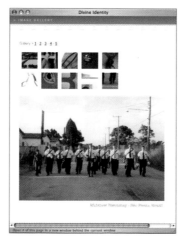

DIVINE IDENTITY WEB SITE ‡ *(This Page)* and **POSTER SERIES** ‡ *(Opposite Page)* **Art Direction/Design/Photography/Copy:** Erik Adams

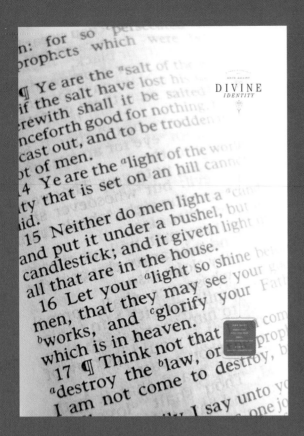

All too often, design is done in a state of stress, hurry, disregard, ambivalence, and disenchantment. When one becomes "disenchanted" with religion, it means enchantment is missing. Yet could there be anything more enchanting than one's belief in an ever-present God, heaven, angels, spirits, or souls? Suppose it is really true that this human experience we all share is about being connected by some universal force. Or imagine one's human response to an encounter with a real angel, a formidable, luminous, winged wonder. The viewer would be awestruck, moved to tears, unable to stand or utter a word. Religions are built upon images of transcendent, incomprehensible grandeur, yet one would never know it by the means through which their stories are so often delivered. With all of our modern day self-empowerment activities, we humans seem to have forgotten that we can still be moved by beliefs and images of the divine. In fact, we must prepare to be moved if we are to engage our modern day crises with any authority or conviction.

The graphic designers and communicators within religion today must work harder to reinvigorate their content and their stories, to recharge their images, to find fresh new ways to open up the symbols of their faith. Where is the ebullience in today's faith-based communications? Where is the sense of the unknowable, the resplendence, the silence, the bliss, the kind of hope you feel at your core? Dialogue between theologians and graphic designers can play an essential role in helping reconnect religious communicators with a dimension of this mystical enchantment, to create works that are able to "bear the weight of the mystery, awe, reverence, and wonder that the liturgical action expresses." [50]

Just as there are many designers who lack a religious or theological perspective, there are many religious communicators who lack sufficient training and experience with respect to design, production, branding, and aesthetics. Graphic design is an applied art form best understood by those who practice it on a daily basis. Religious leaders must be willing to reach out to the design community to learn about and expand upon their visions of what may be possible. The designer must be viewed not as an order taker or as a mere production resource but as a strategic partner who can help shape and elevate perceptions while adding relevant value.

50. United States Conference of Catholic Bishops, *Built of Living Stones: Art, Architecture, and Worship* (Washington, DC: Publications Office, USCCB, 2000), 51.

"There is a sense in which doing aesthetics is not so much a theological option as a theological necessity. The question is only whether it will be done consciously and well."

— Frank Burch Brown, *Religious Aesthetics: A Theological Study of Making and Meaning*, 36.

BIBLICAL WAY OF THE CROSS

Client: GIA Publications **Agency:** KantorGroup
Art Direction: Daniel Kantor **Design:** Kristy Logan
Illustration: Nicholas Markell **Copy:** David Haas

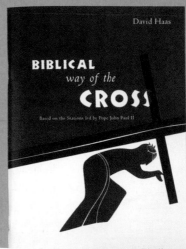

David Haas

BIBLICAL *way of the* **CROSS**

Based on the Stations led by Pope John Paul II

Music by David Haas and Marty Haugen
Images by Nicholas Markell

8

THE EIGHTH STATION
Jesus Is Helped by Simon of Cyrene

Our only hope today lies in our ability to recapture the revolutionary spirit and go out into a sometimes hostile world declaring eternal hostility to poverty, racism, and militarism. (Martin Luther King, Jr.)

INTRODUCTION

Leader   The Eighth Station: Jesus Is Helped by Simon of Cyrene.

RESPONSE

All

We hold the death of the Lord   deep in our hearts.

Liv-ing, now we re-main with Je-sus the Christ.

Copyright © 1983 by GIA Publications, Inc. All rights reserved.

Leader   Please be seated. *(pause)*
          Let us now hear, listen, and receive the gift of God's Word.

10

THE TENTH STATION
Jesus Is Crucified

Love him totally who gave himself totally for your love. (St. Claire of Assisi)

INTRODUCTION

Leader   The Tenth Station: Jesus Is Crucified.

RESPONSE

All

We hold the death of the Lord   deep in our hearts.

Liv-ing, now we re-main with Je-sus the Christ.

Copyright © 1983 by GIA Publications, Inc. All rights reserved.

Leader   Please be seated. *(pause)*
          Let us now hear, listen, and receive the gift of God's Word.

The Tenth Station 47

PRAYER AND PRAXIS

Anyone who has been involved in the development of communications media or practiced graphic design knows it can be a stressful activity. Maintaining focus and mindfulness on any one project can be a challenge, especially when simultaneously working for multiple clients, religious and secular. Any designer performing faith-oriented work could draw inspiration from the prayer and praxis of the illuminators and iconographers. To these artisans, there is virtually no distinction between praying and working. Before any work begins, a process comprised of three deepening forms of prayer is engaged, including external prayer, which builds trust in the senses and the imagination; inner prayer, which fills one's heart with godlike richness; and the mind-heart prayer or monotonous prayer, which involves maintaining vigilant attention to the stillness of both mind and heart throughout the entire process of conceiving a work.

This alignment of prayer with action is built upon the belief that one can only work from a peaceful state of mind and heart. "Discipline and control are needed in order that, with each brush stroke, the mind and heart would be united by the mysterious awareness of knowing God to be present. The inner prayer creates a center of peace in the heart regardless of intrusions by worldly winds."[51] Concept and intention are held in suspension while artist, theologian, writer, spirit, and God become one.

When persons create an icon, they are often said to be writing it, since the word iconography literally means "image writing." There are many iconographic traditions. Some focus on a mystical approach, for what is being expressed is prayer-art or a mind-heart prayer. The process begins with a prayer, which is first verbally, though silently spoken. This prayer is reflected upon through the mind and finally directed toward the heart. The prayer is then "pronounced" again through the resulting image. Mind, heart, action, and prayer become one. "Prayer is a form of iconwriting performed in the mind and heart. The practice of prayer is the same as iconwriting because both of them are liturgical and involve many progressive steps of ascent toward perceiving the Divine. God in reality is becoming depicted in the soul of the praying person in the same sense as He is depicted through the symbols of color, light, and linear perspective."[52]

In the middle ages, the illuminators similarly believed that their actions were united with prayer. God as maker was revealed through human as maker, both desiring to be approached through shared reality, abundance, and beauty. The graphic designers today

51. Vladislav Andrejev, *Iconwriter's Daily Prayer* (New York: Prosopon School of Iconology, 2002), 2.

52. Ibid., 1.

NATIVITY CHRISTMAS CARD, CA. 1960 Client: Nazareth Hall Seminary, St. Paul **Design:** Frank Kacmarcik

MANGER CHRISTMAS CARD, CA. 1960 Client: Alfred and Florence Muellerleile **Design:** Frank Kacmarcik

Photos: © The Hill Museum & Manuscript Library, Arca Artium collection, St. John's University

255

who are charged with the task of giving form and substance to many of today's religious communications can learn from these traditions. The romantic ideal of using ancient materials need not be considered more sacred than engaging in the tremendous gift of modern technology. It is possible, even in an age when graphic design is so technologically dependent, to realign one's actions with one's beliefs. It is possible to see a new laser printer or a large-screen monitor as a gift of creation through which work of the divine may be done. But if graphic design is to be prayer-like, practiced and approached as if a sacred vocation, or treated with the same respect as iconwriting or illumination, it requires getting beyond ourselves, our technologies, and our egos. Only then can we experience a renewed sense of wonder with it all. Only then can we tap our abilities to subordinate our efforts to something beyond ourselves and beyond that which we create.

GRAPHIC DESIGN AS METAPHOR

Designers have the power to unify and empower the multitude of messages and media produced by faith-based organizations today—this is accomplished not through their technical skill, but through their ability to ideate, to imagine, and to dream of a whole whose parts resonate with a sense of the sacred. Only when design becomes prayer can this happen. Creativity finds its ultimate origin in God—and humans, blessed with the ability to express this creativity, do so through deliberate engagements of the senses. Many religions view the creation of beauty as participating in the goodness of the Creator, a godlike activity that brings us closer to the divine and its revelation.

Painting, architecture, dance, and textiles are some of the modes of expression in the human quest for meaning. When viewed through a theological lens, every art form offers the gift of its own window into divinity. Consider music, for example, a medium experienced in most formal worship environments. Theologian Father Jan Michael Joncas sees music as "a medium that confronts humans with the intangible. Music makes time audible for humans insofar as all perception of sound involves an experience of impermanence, acoustic events that come into and go out of existence; this characteristic correlates with the theological claim of the historical character of the created order and the eternal God who really relates to it."[53] Thus, from a theological perspective, music may be seen as correlative of God as an elusive presence.

53. In J. G. Davies, ed., *The New Westminster Dictionary of Liturgy and Worship* (Philadelphia: Westminster Press, 1986), 326.

REVELATIONS CHRISTMAS CARD Client: Nazareth Hall Seminary, St. Paul   Design/Illustration: Frank Kacmarcik
Photo: © The Hill Museum & Manuscript Library, Arca Artium collection, St. John's University

How might graphic design be viewed theologically? What are its unique offerings? How might theologians contrast the unique gifts of graphic design with those of other art forms? In a broad sense, graphic design is a coalescent medium in which otherwise independent elements, such as letters, words, illustrations, photography, symbols, textures, colors, and materials become wholly united and subordinated to a higher order. Designers are commonly required to accommodate and unify component parts from many other artists and contributors. A good designer must serve as both composer and conductor, choosing which elements to amplify, which to harmonize, and which must play a supporting role. Graphic design shares much of music's need for paced delivery and for the ordering of events through spatial time and linear time.

Visual communications that exhibit honesty, hope, and ordered meaning in this disordered world have the power to mirror the human narrative of creation, falling, and redemption. Graphic design's power to bring order to chaos may be best realized when seen as both theology as well as a vehicle to carry its message. When designing, one participates through thought and interaction in the ordering of the divine logos. It is an intensely collaborative activity—serving as nexus, graphic design becomes a powerful metaphor for unity, creation, and reason.

Just as independent musicians and instruments come together in an ensemble, contributors from many disciplines are able to gather through graphic design. Writers, illustrators, painters, typographers, and photographers all find a common home in graphic design. Efforts made to unify the works of so many echo the many scriptural symbols of vines, branches, trees, and roots—symbols that become metaphors for unity, many-to-one, common source, and coming together. Graphic design is a medium that echoes these themes. Many messages of faith also profess the need for humility, generosity, and selflessness. These are qualities inherent to the practice of good graphic design. Through the medium of graphic design, the disparate works of many are made whole through a single, unified image.

While graphic designers serving religion must strive for their works to be inwardly unifying, they must also emphasize outward unification. When a family of works is made cohesive through a common voice, the viewer is able to experience the summative effect of humility unified. Graphic design is an art form rarely practiced in solitude for oneself. People with diverse skill sets are required to work within their areas of expertise

Logos is Greek for "word," "reason," and "ratio." It represents the divine reason that acts as the ordering principle of the universe. Medieval philosophers and theologians believed that one partook in the *Divine Logos* while thinking or reasoning.

OLD PINE MINISTRY PAMPHLETS[‡] **Client:** Old Pine Street Presbyterian Church **Agency:** JoToGo **Art Direction/Design:** Jody Graff
Illustration: Gertrud Mueller Nelson

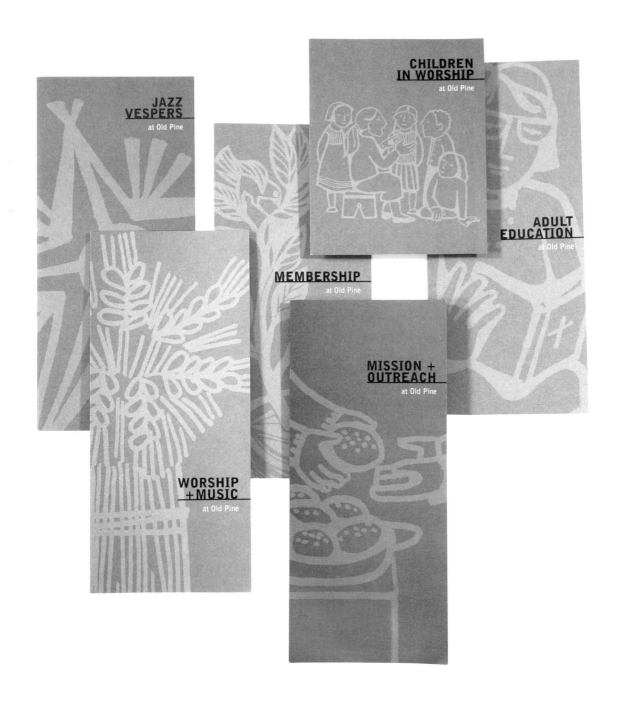

When a family of works is made cohesive through a common voice, the viewer is able to experience the summative effect of humility unified.

54. Dyrness, *Visual Faith*, 128.

while remaining in dialogue with each other. The pervasive media forms that so powerfully influence contemporary society, such as TV, Internet, video games, and software, share graphic design's collaborative nature. "Today there seems to be an openness, one might say a longing, to work together in making experiences and objects that move and delight audiences." [54] Graphic design is an art form that becomes a visual witness of the need for isolated realities to come together through integration, team building, and bridge building. Few other art forms are able to bring such diversity of expressions together. To participate in graphic design is to participate in a living symbol of concord made manifest.

THIS BOOK IS ONLY A BEGINNING

For creative professionals to commit themselves to this specialty and for faith-based clients to increase their demand for graphic design services, bridges need to be built. This means graphic designers need to reach out to the religious community and vice versa. Neither can benefit from the other while in isolation. It is up to those who desire a more beautiful way of communicating with and through faith to elevate religious messages.

It will also require forethought with respect to budgeting. Design fees always seem high to organizations that view graphic design as an unnecessary expense or as a low-priority production task. When viewed strategically, however, design offers value propositions that can far outweigh its costs. This may require inviting a designer to your table sooner rather than later. Waiting until the last minute almost always costs more and delivers less.

Designers and religious communicators are called to illuminate and reimagine new standards for today's religious media. Each worship tradition will have its own point of view, its own history, its own visual ancestry to draw from. Design in service of religion may be seen as a continuation of all the great design servants who have gone before us. It is an art form that represents an opportunity to stand up for the honesty of beauty and the truthfulness of form. It is the delivery vehicle through which proud, rich stories may be told and through which those who experience them may be moved and blessed.

(All) **ADE BETHUNE IMAGES** **Illustration:** Ade Bethune
Ade Bethune Collection, College of St. Catherine Library, St. Paul, Minnesota.

1. TWO HEARTS IN ONE
2. KING OF KINGS, LORD OF LORDS
3. CULTIVATING THE GARDEN OF THE HEART
4. THE TREE OF LIFE

Resources

American Institute of Graphic Arts (AIGA)

AIGA, a professional association for design, is committed to furthering excellence in design as a broadly defined discipline, a strategic tool for business, and a cultural force. Design professionals turn to AIGA to exchange ideas and information, to participate in critical analysis and research, and to advance education and ethical practice. AIGA is a national organization with many state and local chapters, which you can connect to from their Web site, www.aiga.org.

AIGA also offers helpful documents to designers free of charge. Any of these documents may be downloaded as PDF files from the AIGA Web site at http://www.aiga. org/content.cfm/designbusinessandethics. Document subjects include:

- *Client's guide to design:* a great resource for anyone wanting to learn more about how to work with a graphic designer.

- *Business and ethical expectations for professional designers:* an overview of the standards of professional conduct that reflect the best interests of the profession, the client, and the viewing public.

- *Use of fonts:* an overview of the legal and moral issues of using or sharing fonts, which are considered intellectual property.

- *Use of illustrations:* an overview of ethical and professional concerns pertaining to the use of original illustrations.

- *Use of software:* a review of how licensing is different from purchasing and why it is essential to understand the rights of the user as well as the software publisher.

- *Guide to copyright:* a guide to the laws the pertain to working with intellectual property such as original art, illustration, photography, and software.

- *Use of photography:* a comprehensive guide on the options available to designers when considering use of original or stock photography; a review of the photographer's intellectual property rights.

- *Sales tax:* an introduction to tax liabilities and requirements.

- *Print design and environmental responsibility:* the relationship between graphic design and its effects on the ecological environment.

- *AIGA standard form of agreement for design services:* the process of drafting, negotiating, and finalizing a client agreement, helpful for both designers and clients.

Arca Artium, St. John's University

Arca Artium, or "Ark of the Arts," is a collection of rare works that are part of the Hill Museum and Manuscript Library (HMML) of St. John's University in Collegeville, Minnesota. Developed from the working collection of Frank Kacmarcik (1920–2004), teacher, liturgical designer, graphic artist, typographer, and calligrapher, Arca Artium's areas of interest focus on the book arts, graphic art, liturgical art, and architecture. Its rare book library and fine art print holdings anchor Arca Artium. These two collection components each number more than four thousand items that are meant to serve generations of students. For more information, visit http://www.hmml.org/arca/arca.htm.

The Ade Bethune Collection, College of St. Catherine Library

Ade Bethune contributed much to the fields of sacred art & architecture and social justice as an artist, writer, and liturgical consultant. Her leadership covered over half a century of significant work, all flowing from her early association with Dorothy Day and the publication of her pictures in The Catholic Worker. Many of here images are available for use today through The College of St. Catherine, St. Paul, Minnesota. For more information, visit http://library.stkate.edu/spcoll/bethune.html.

Christians in the Visual Arts (CIVA)

CIVA explores the relationship between the visual arts and the Christian faith. Founded in 1979, CIVA first met to consider the place of the Christian artist in the church and in the world at large. Their Web site is www.civa.org.

The Spirit Source

Some of the finest professional artists working in the religious and spiritual genre today are represented through this Web site of stock imagery. All of the images are rights-managed and they make purchases quite easy. Visit www.thespiritsource.com.

Society for Environmental Graphic Design (SEGD)

SEGD is an international nonprofit educational organization providing resources for design specialists in the field of environmental graphic design, architecture, and landscape, interior, and industrial design. SEGD members typically design directional and attraction sign systems, destination graphics, identity programs, exhibits, and themed environments. Their Web site is www.segd.org.

Society of American Graphic Artists (SAGA)

SAGA reflects the growth and changes taking place in printmaking as well as transformations in the larger world of art. SAGA features national exhibitions of American printmaking. Their Web site is www.clt.astate.edu/elind/sagamain.htm.

The Art Directors Club (ADC)

ADC is an organization for integrated media and the first international creative collective of its kind. Founded in New York in 1920, the ADC is a self-funding nonprofit organization that celebrates and inspires creative excellence in visual communication. Its mission is to promote the highest standards of excellence and integrity in visual communications and to encourage students and young professionals entering the field. Their Web site is www.adcglobal.org.

The Graphic Artists Guild

The Graphic Artists Guild is a national union of illustrators, designers, web creators, production artists, surface designers, and other creative professionals. Membership is open to all working artists. Every guild member is guaranteed a voice and the opportunity to actively participate. The Graphic Artists Guild Web site is www.gag.org.

The National Council of Churches USA: Communication Commission

The Communication Commission is one of the five program commissions of the National Council of Churches USA, the leading organization for ecumenical cooperation among Christian denominations in the United States. The Commission's members are professional communicators who work in print, broadcast, film, Web, news, media relations and other communication tasks, usually on the national level. Their Web site is www.ncccusa.org/about/communication.html

SELECTED BIBLIOGRAPHY

Design

Felici, James. *The Complete Manual of Typography: A Guide to Setting Perfect Type.* Berkeley, CA: Peachpit Press, 2003.

Grear, Malcolm. *Inside/Outside: From the Basics to the Practice of Design.* New York: Van Nostrand Reinhold, 1993.

Napoles, Veronica. *Corporate Identity Design.* New York: Van Nostrand Reinhold, 1988.

Ortbal, John, Mike Lange, and Michael S. Carroll. *The Ecology of Design.* New York: The AIGA Press, 1996.

Rand, Paul. *Design, Form, and Chaos.* New Haven: Yale University Press, 1993.

———. *From Lascaux to Brooklyn.* New Haven: Yale University Press, 1996.

———. *Paul Rand: A Designer's Art.* New Haven: Yale University Press, 1985.

Tschihold, Jan. *The Form of the Book: Essays on the Morality of Good Design.* Point Roberts, WA: Harley & Marks, 1991.

Beauty, Theology, and Aesthetics

Avis, Paul. *God and the Creative Imagination: Metaphor, Symbol, and Myth in Religion and Theology.* London and New York: Routledge, 1999.

Boyer, Mark G. *The Liturgical Environment: What the Documents Say.* 2nd ed. Collegeville, MN: The Liturgical Press, 2004.

Brown, Frank Burch. *Good Taste, Bad Taste, and Christian Taste: Aesthetics in Religious Life.* New York: Oxford University Press, 2000.

———. *Religious Aesthetics: A Theological Study of Making and Meaning.* Princeton: Princeton University Press, 1989.

Harries, Richard. *Art and the Beauty of God.* New York and London: Mowbray, 1994.

McDannell, Colleen. *Material Christianity: Religion and Popular Culture in America.* New Haven: Yale University Press, 1995.

Miles, Margaret R. *Image as Insight: Visual Understanding in Western Christianity and Secular Culture.* Boston: Beacon Press, 1985.

O'Donohue, John. *Beauty, the Invisible Embrace.* New York: HarperCollins Publishers, 2004. (audio: Sounds True, Boulder, CO, 2004).

Philibert, Paul, and Frank Kacmarcik. *Seeing and Believing.* Collegeville, MN: The Liturgical Press, 1995.

Tillich, Paul. *On Art and Architecture.* Edited with an introduction by John Dillenberger in collaboration with Jane Dillenberger. Translations from German texts by Robert P. Scharlemann. New York: Crossroad, 1987.

United States Council of Catholic Bishops. *Built of Living Stones: Art, Architecture, and Worship.* Washington, DC: Publications Office, USCCB, 2000.

————. *Environment and Art in Catholic Worship.* Washington, DC: Publications Office, USCCB, 1978.

Viladesau, Richard. *Theology and the Arts: Encountering God through Music, Art, and Rhetoric.* New York: Paulist Press, 2000.

Illuminations

Alexander, Jonathan James Graham. *Medieval Illuminators and Their Methods of Work.* New Haven: Yale University Press, 1992.

Diringer, David. *The Illuminated Book: Its History and Production.* New York: Philosophical Library, 1958.

Theophilus. *On Divers Arts: The Foremost Medieval Treatise on Paintings, Glassmaking, and Metalwork.* Translated from the Latin with an introduction and notes by John G. Hawthorne and Cyril Stanley Smith. New York: Dover Publications, 1979.

Watson, Rowan. *Illuminated Manuscripts and Their Makers.* London: V & A Publications; New York: Harry N. Abrams, 2003.

Symbols

Dilasser, Maurice. *The Symbols of the Church.* Translated by Mary Cabrin, Madeleine Beaumont, and Caroline Morson. Collegeville, MN: The Liturgical Press, 1999.

Dillistone, F. W. *The Power of Symbols in Religion and Culture.* New York: Crossroad, 1986.

Frutiger, Adrain. *Signs and Symbols: Their Design and Meaning.* Translated by Andrew Bluhm. New York: Watson-Guptill Publications, 1998.

Index of Images

by Agency or Artist

About the Author

DANIEL KANTOR is the founder, principal, and creative director of KantorGroup, an award-winning strategic brand communications consultancy serving a broad range of national corporate clients, including organizations such as GIA Publications and Augsburg Fortress. KantorGroup was the principal design consultant for *Evangelical Lutheran Worship* pew edition, the core resource used by the Evangelical Lutheran Church in America. Kantor is also a published liturgical music composer, whose works include the best-selling Christmas classic "Night of Silence," which is in widespread use throughout the world.

For more information visit www.danielkantor.com.